# FUMIO DEMURA
*In His Own Words*

By
Jose M. Fraguas

Jose M. Fraguas
EMPIRE BOOKS/AWP LLC
Los Angeles, California

**INGRAM**
**Disclaimer**
Please note that the author and publisher of this book are NOT RESPONSIBLE in any manner whatsoever for any injury that may result from practicing the techniques and/or following the instructions given within. Since the physical activities described herein may be too strenuous in nature for some readers to engage in safely, it is essential that a physician be consulted prior to training.

First Edition published in 2024 by AWP LLC/Empire Books.

All rights reserved. No part of this publication may be reproduced or utilized in any form or by any means, electronic or mechanical, including photo - copying, recording, or by any information storage and retrieval system, without prior written permission from AWP LLC/Empire Books.

EMPIRE BOOKS
P.O. Box 491788
Los Angeles, CA 90049

First edition
Library of Congress Catalog Number: ISBN-13: 978-1-949753-62-2
24 23 22 21 20 19 18 17 16 15 14 13 12
Library of Congress Cataloging-in-Publication Data
In his own words Fumio Demura / by Jose M. Fraguas. -- 1st revised ed. p. cm. Includes index.

ISBN 978-1-949753-62-2 (pbk.: alk. paper)
1. Karate. 5. Martial arts--philosophy. 3. Large type books. I. Title.
GV1222.3.F715 23341924.715'3--dc24
2006006643.

Printed in the United States of America.

"I believe that a true traditional Karate-do instructor should teach his students the morality of Martial Arts and a sense of knightliness that should be felt in everything he does."

- **Fumio Demura**

# Dedication

I dedicate this book to the memory of Fumio Demura Sensei.

# Acknowledgments

Many people were responsible for making this book possible, some more directly than others. I want to extend my gratitude to all those whom so generously contributed their time and experience to the preparation of this work in an effort to preserve the legacy of Fumio Demura Sensei.

To all the instructors under Demura Sensei lineage, whom share the art of karate with their students around the world. The "Fumio Demura" legacy lives on thanks to you.

You all have my enduring thanks.

— Jose M. Fraguas

# About the Author

Born and raised in Madrid, Spain, Jose M. Fraguas began his martial arts studies with judo, in grade school, at age 9. From there he moved to study Shito Ryu karate-do under his teacher, Masahiro Okada Sensei, eventually receiving a seventh-degree black belt and the Shihan certifi- cate from Soke K. Mabuni. He began his career as a writer at age 16 as a regular contributor to martial arts magazines in Great Britain, France, Spain, Italy, Germany, Portugal, Holland and Australia. In 1980, he moved to Los Angeles, California, where his open-minded mentality helped him to develop a more elaborated approach to the martial arts.

Fraguas founded his first publishing company in Europe, authoring dozens of books and distributing his magazines to 35 countries in three different languages. His reputation and credibility as a martial artist and publisher became well known to the top masters around the world. Considering himself a martial artist first and a writer and publisher second, Fraguas feels fortunate to have had the opportunity to interview many legendary martial artists. He recognizes that much of the information given in the interviews helped him to discover new dimensions in the martial arts. "I was constantly absorbing knowledge from the great masters," he recalls. "I only trained with a few of them, but intellectually, academically and spiritually all of them have made very important contributions to my growth as a complete martial artist."

Steeped in tradition yet looking to the future, Fraguas understands and appreciates martial arts history and philosophy and feels this rich heritage is a necessary steppingstone to personal growth and spiritual evolution. His desire to promote both ancient philosophy and modern thinking provides the motivation for his writing. "If the motivation is just money, a book cannot be of good quality," Fraguas says. "If the book is written to just make people happy, it cannot be deep. I want to write books so I can learn as well as teach. Karate-do, like human life itself, is filled with experiences that seem quite ordinary at the time and assume a fabled stature only with the passage of the years. I hope this work will be useful for future practitioners to appreciate the great legacy of Fumio Demura Sensei.

It is clear that every one of us will some kind of leave a legacy behind when we die. The challenge is the same for all of us. For Fraguas, who has authored more than 35 books, the important question is what kind of legacy will I leave? "I believe our main legacy as writers is to educate or even just re-echo those things that we believe are worthwhile - a subjective matter. Even If the idea is obvious or simple, we believe it deserves to be kept alive, and we do that using different ways current with the times; we broadcast our worldview with our  family, friends, co-workers, and so on," he says. "Ideally we live by our beliefs so as to lend them credence; the "unfollowing adherent" is just a meaningless mouthpiece - a preacher not following his own sermon. A legacy of values proven out by the bearer's own life would be a very good legacy for anyone. Life is motion, and the real goal of a writer should be to arrest that motion [which is life] and preserve knowledge [the words of Demura Sensei in this book] by artificial means, and hold it fixed so that a hundred years later, when a stranger opens a book and reads it, it moves again since it is life. Since man is mortal, the only immortality possible for a writer is to leave something behind him that is immortal since it will always move. This is the writer's way of scribbling "I was here" on the wall of the final and irrevocable oblivion through which we all must someday pass."

Jose M. Fraguas lives in Los Angeles, California.

# TABLE OF CONTENTS

**INTRODUCTION** ............................... X

**ONE ON ONE INTERVIEW** ........ XII

**SENSEI FUMIO DEMURA KARATE TECHNIQUES** ................ 56

    SHOULDER GRAB ................................. 58
    DOUBLE LAPEL GRAB ......................... 59
    NECK GRAB (TWO HANDS) ............... 60
    CROSSED WRIST GRAB (1) ................ 61
    CROSSED WRIST GRAB (2) ............... 62
    BEAR HUG ............................................ 63
    FRONT TACKLE ................................... 64

**FACE OFF** .................................................. **66**

**ADDENDUM** ............................................. **68**

### KENWA MABUNI
THE FOUNDER OF SHITO RYU .......... 70

### RYUSHO SAKAGAMI
THE GENTLE MASTER ......................... 78

### DAN IVAN
KARATE'S ENDURING SPIRIT ............ 80

### SHIGERU SAWABE
A LEGACY OF EXCELLENCE .............. 100

# Introduction

Born in Yokohama, Japan in 1940, Fumio Demura was a martial arts superstar. The All-Japan Karate Champion in 1961, began training in kendo and karate at age eight in his hometown with Mr. Asano, and then started karate, kendo, and iaido training with Ryusho Sakagami and Taisaburo Nakamura at age 13. Sensei Demura came to United States in 1965 to share his knowledge and spread his teachings in his own unique exuberant way. In so doing, he managed the difficult task of preserving the old values passed to him by his Japanese masters without compromising his traditional beliefs.

Amongst his accomplishments he was the kumite finalist, 1960 East Japan Karate Championships. Winner of the first, and finalist of the third, All-Japan Karate Fighting Championships in 1961 and 1963, respectively. Kumite finalist in the All-Japan Shito-Ryu Championships, 1964. "Black Belt" Magazine Instructor of the Year, 1969. "Golden Fist" Award winner for Outstanding Instructor, 1973. "Black Belt" Magazine Man of the Year, 1975 and authored many books on karate and kobudo and appeared in many movies since then.

Within ten years of his arrival in the U.S., Fumio Demura had broken the traditional ban on public demonstrations, and started a successful chain of karate schools.

He was not only a superb technician and a great martial artist but one of the finest performers and weapons experts in the world as well. Credited with being the first professional karate performer to incorporate lights, music, costumes, and martial arts into the same routine, his technical prowess was breathtaking – as was the trademark precision of his punches and kicks. Expanding his sphere of influence, this true renaissance man went on to appear in a succession of movies with such stars as Burt Lancaster, Pat Morita, and Sean Connery. Easy going and affable, he was one of the most accessible Karate masters to learn from.

Fumio Demura was without a doubt, one of the most famous and highly respected martial artists around the world. Sensei Demura's reputation was the result of more than four decades years of dedication and hard work. His constant need to challenge himself did earn him wide acclaim. He was been featured on more than 60 magazine covers worldwide, written a number of best-selling books and authored two classical series of DVD for "Ancient Warrior Productions" about Shito Ryu Karate and Okinawa Kobudo.

A modern martial artist firmly rooted in tradition, Fumio Demura Sensei lived life on his own terms and was one of traditional karate's most popular and important figures in the history of the art around the world.

*By Jose M. Fraguas*

# ONE ON ONE

*with*

# FUMIO DEMURA

1

# IN HIS OWN WORDS

### Sensei, when you did get born and who were your parents?

I was born on September 15, 1940 in Yokohama, Kanagawa, Japan My father was Hitoshi Demura and my mother Masu Kawashima.

### What do you remember of your early days in Japan as a kid?

The memories are many and they feel now like a "movie"…like something so far in the past that it is hard to believe that "it was me" who lived those things many years ago.

As a child I was weak, I did not have a strong body and exercises like many may think of me. It was the Martial Arts training that actually started to change my body and made me stronger. Martial Arts was something that I enjoyed to do, therefore it was not "difficult" to go to the dojo and train. Little by little my body changed and I developed confidence in myself. It was a process that took years but definitely changed and defined my life for the years to come.

### As a child, did you have an outgoing personality?

My personality as a child was very different from what it is now. I was very bashful and it was almost impossible for me to go in front of people. From a physical point of view, I was very weak kid; I had a problem with my tonsils. Fortunately, Martial Arts changed all that.

### When did you start training in Karate?

It was a long time ago. I started training because of illness. As a child, I got a severe infection in my tonsils as I just Said, which left me very weak. The doctor Said I should exercise a little. When I was 8 years old, I started taking kendo lessons under Sensei Asano. When he had to move away, he gave me a

# One-on-One with Fumio Demura

letter of recommendation for Ryusho Sakagami to begin Karate training. But I didn't take it seriously until I was around 12 years old. Then, I also studied aikido, kyudo, and judo during my high school days. I went to high school to study drama because I wanted to be an actor. But once I finished school, my father disapproved my choice so I had to go to the University to study Economics because that's what my father wanted me to do.

### How was your early training in Japan like?

In the beginning, it was very different because tournament sparring had not yet really taken off. Our training was primarily for self-defense and the techniques directed to the eyes, throat, and groin were emphasized – things we could use in an actual street-fight. After the first JKA championships were held in 1957, and I went to see them, I began to think about training in a different way, with the idea of tournaments more in mind. The stances and techniques changed, and we began to concentrate on gyaku-zuki (reverse punch) and mae-geri (front kick).

### Were you a natural at Karate?

No, not really. One thing that we have to remember is that Karate is not a "natural" thing for the body to do. We need to "teach" the body to move in the "Karate way", like learning a new language. You must "educate" your body to move the way the style describe and that takes time and dedication. Let's not forget that the "physical talent" that makes things look "natural" is based on the genetics of the practitioner. Some have great genetics for swimming – body type, body fat percentage, long limbs, etc…and these factor make that this specific individual be more "natural" at swimming.

Karate is different. Karate is for everybody and as long as you display the fundamental principles of the technique, the way it looks from the outside is not as important as the effectiveness of the movement. But to answer your question directly, the answer is "no". I worked hard to make my technique the way it supposed to be. That is the traditional way.

### What's your rank in Karate-do?

Rank is something I really don't care about, but because you asked I hold a 9th Dan in shito ryu Karate-do. Today, everybody wants recognition; everybody wants to be called "master." They say, "They don't give credit to me." I really feel embarrassed by all this for the sake of the art of Karate-do and Martial Arts.

# IN HIS OWN WORDS

**So you think they are not really important?**

They are important to a certain extent. Traditionally, we had only white, brown and black belt. We started to use different colors after the idea was introduced in the art of Judo by founder Jigoro Kano. And I think it made a lot of sense. Each belt represents a step in the ladder to obtain the black belt level. If we go from white belt to black belt it will take a long time and it is a long journey, but creating a series of "goals" along the way, the student can focus more efficiently in one step at a time. The next goal is right in front of him or her and makes it easier to tackle the task. What the student has to understand is that each promotion is not an end in itself but simply the beginning for the next step. There is an important feeling of accomplishment when you get a new belt and that should be used to keep pushing forward in your journey. At the same time the periods between belts should be reasonable for the students to keep themselves motivated and focused on the goal.

**How did you come to study Kobudo?**

Thanks to Sensei Sakagami, I was able to receive my training from Kenshin Taira, a legendary Kobudo master who died in 1973. Master Sakagami invited him to become a teacher in our dojo and he accepted the position and came to live in Master Sakagami's house. Master Taira influenced a lot of people because he was moving around all the time in order to teach the art. Due to his age, Sensei Taira was a little hard to communicate with – but his skill and teaching abilities were fantastic. He was a typical "old-style" sensei and taught just one way, which never ever changed. He was very, very special. Master Sakagami also was a kendo and iaido teacher. I took iaido and kendo classes from him, but I also trained kendo under Sensei Taisaburo Nakamura.

**What did Sensei Sakagami mean to you?**

Everything. Master Ryusho Sakagami had a big influence on my life and was like a second father to me. He was a guide not only as a Karate master but also as a "father figure". I really looked up to him. While he didn't physically train me so much because he was old, he was always there supervising the training and making sure everything was going in the right direction. I enjoyed his company and admired him very much so in a sense you can say that he helped to "shape" who Fumio Demura is today.

**So you study other Martial Arts?**

Yes, I did but because of my attitude toward rank, I never tested for belts in them. I was never interested in degrees and ranks so I focused only on train-

## One-on-One with Fumio Demura

ing and learning. I understand that rank has a place in Martial Arts but it was never my goal. It is true that with time, you realize that in the "real" world these things have a certain amount of value and I came to accept the fact that if you deserve it…you should get it. It is pretty much like if you spend four or five years in Harvard University studying Law. Why not to accept your Degree and Diploma when you graduate? You should! Just remember that a piece of paper do not "define" who your are as a martial artist.

### How was the training during the old days?

Very difficult. The training was harder and very demanding. We used to train the basics every day for hours. Just basics!

### It is true that you failed your first test for white belt?

Yes, I did! In fact, that made me realize a lot of things. It embarrassed me so much that I decided to set goals and put even more time into training. Since then, I have always believed that failures can make you grow and improve if you know how to make a stepping-stone out of them.

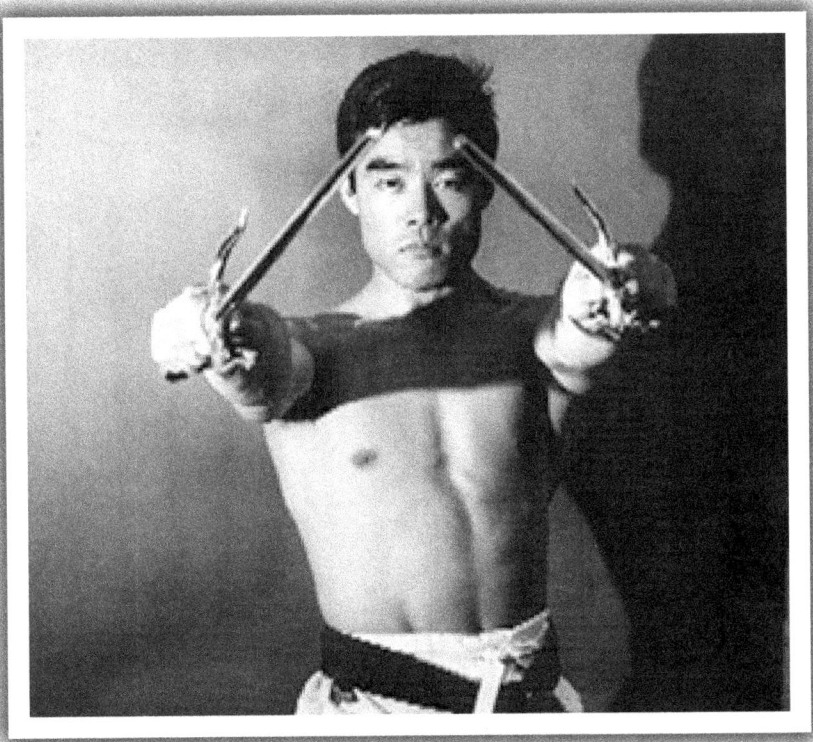

# IN HIS OWN WORDS

### How hard was it to win the All Japan Karate Championship?

That tournament was very hard because every style, association, and school was there – goju ryu, shotokan, shito ryu, wado ryu, etc. It was very difficult to win because the best fighters in Japan were competing in it. I was very nervous. I had fought in other small tournaments but never in a big one like that.

### When did you decide to come to the United States?

The final decision was in 1965, but in 1963 I was helping Sensei Sakagami doing some demonstrations and I've got to meet Don F. Draeger. Mr. Draeger was assisting his jiu-jitsu teacher, Takaji Shimizu, and I was helping Sensei Sakagami. I had no idea that meeting Don would change the course of my life. We became good friends and he later introduced me to Sensei Dan Ivan. I remember that when I arrived to the United States, I had to fight a great battle against frustration because of my poor English. I recall crying in bed for more than two days because I couldn't communicate at all. It was very difficult for me to adapt to a new culture and language. But Ed Parker gave me an opportunity to demonstrate my art of Japanese karate publicly at the 1965 Long Beach International Karate Championships, and that boosted my confidence and self-image.

### How it was the process to come to the U.S.?

It was not really easy even if I had already a sponsor. Getting a Visa not to visit as a tourist but to stay in the United States it was very hard. Thanks to the support of Dan Ivan and a couple of connections I had in the U.S. Embassy in Tokyo, I was able of getting all the paperwork to travel.

### Who was your first connection in California?

Definitely Sensei Dan Ivan. He used to travel to Japan a lot – he was part of the U.S. Intelligence Services and we became very good friends. He brought me over to the U.S. and later offered me a partnership that lasted for a very

# One-on-One with Fumio Demura

long time – not only in Martial Arts but in other different businesses as well, such as real estate. I would say that Dan Ivan, along with Ed Parker, Mito Uyehara and Curtis F. Wong, helped me very, very much.

**Dan Ivan was a shotokan stylist and you are a shito ryu practitioner. How did you combine those two styles?**

Well, out of respect for Ivan Sensei, I learned all the shotokan kata and taught them so the school would have the same curriculum. Many years later, when we separated our ways, I went back to teaching strictly traditional shito ryu and Kobudo.

**How do Westerners respond to traditional Japanese training?**

In the beginning it was hard for me to communicate with the students because I did not speak a word of English so the way my students learnt from me was based on a "visual" format. I tried to correct them with body movements.

If you think about it that is the way traditionally we learn in Japan. The Sensei doesn't go around talking a lot. It is one or two words – if any, and that is!

Therefore the training sessions were focused on developing very strong basics, a lot of "kihon" and for that you do not need too many words.

# IN HIS OWN WORDS

This form of training is very good for beginners but when the students advance, you need to use more verbal communication to explain deeper details in technique.

Eventually I starting it mix both ways and the students developed properly in their Karate journey.

### Have you made any innovations to the styles you trained in?

Who hasn't? Everybody makes innovation to what they are practicing or teaching compared to what they learned in the past. Even all the great Martial Arts masters did. Who thinks Jigoro Kano, Gichin Funakoshi or Morihei Ueshiba taught exactly what was passed on to them by their teachers? They were very traditional in the sense that they kept cultural values such as respect, moral and work ethics alive and didn't concentrate strictly on physical techniques. Innovations should be made based on realistic and functional experiences.

### Did you ever meet Bruce Lee?

Yes. He was very nice to me. Bruce had a very strong sense for everything related to Martial Arts. He always wanted to learn more and never was satisfied with what he had. I remember that after my book on Nunchaku came out, he would call me up with questions about the weapon, which he was studying at that time.

### What it was your opinion of him at that time and now?

He was a great guy and was very fast. I couldn't believe how fast he was at that time and how hard he could hit. His secret was that what he did know, he knew very well. He was able to use it in combat. He never made the mistake of accumulating a lot of things. It was very difficult to estimate his whole knowledge, because he always looked for the quality of what he was doing not the quantity.

# One-on-One with Fumio Demura

**❝**In the beginning it was hard for me to communicate with the students because I did not speak a word of English so the way my students learnt from me was based on a "visual" format. I tried to correct them with body movements.**❞**

# IN HIS OWN WORDS

He was a very talented martial artist. I think he perceived at a very early stage that the way the Martial Arts were being taught it was not the most efficient way in order to give the students the tool for self-defense. I agreed with him. A lot of philosophy made a lot of sense to me at that time. He wanted to train more efficiently using equipment, like a boxer, and also for the kicking techniques with the kicking shield and other pieces of equipment.

He had a very open mind to new ideas and ways to develop his body and train his techniques. He never appeared to me like someone who was willing to fully stick to tradition and allow his Martial Arts to stay in the past.

He was concerned about his body and truly believed that the body was the "real secret". This is very true; if you are not in shape and in a good physical condition, you may know 1,000 of techniques but you won't be able of efficiently use a single one!

**Sensei, are there any 'secret' techniques in Karate like some people mention?**

This is a question that many people around the world always ask. Let me simply say that there are no 'secret' techniques. The 'advanced' techniques are those we use in a real fight. There are no 'secret' moves or applications that will defeat any other technique. Basic techniques are the ones we should use in real fights…therefore these 'basic' techniques are the true secret of our training. Karate and Martial Arts expertise in general is based on how you can put these basic and fundamental moves into a practical application under several different circumstances.

**Your approach to the Martial Arts seems to be very different and open-minded compared to other traditional masters.**

I consider myself a traditionalist because I maintain the ethical and moral principles of the art as they were passed to me. From the technical point of view I tried to evolve with the times and make the art useful for modern times. This is a concept that many teachers misunderstand. The styles of Martial Arts are based on what was useful at a certain period of time. The physical techniques were suitable for that particular moment in history. Everything evolves and the environment and circumstances change as well. Therefore, the techniques have to adapt the new environment. There is nothing wrong with this. Look at the car racing technology. The cars are not the same as they were 15 or 20 years ago. The driving skills have changed because the cars have changed. The cars are faster and new skills and knowledge of physics and aerodynamics are necessary to bring out the most of both cars and drivers. The physical training for the drivers has changed as well. Do you see how improvement and evolution affects the whole car racing world? Well, it is the same with the Martial Arts. The problem is that some people want to stick to those things that are not useful anymore.

**You were one of the first to use music to display traditional Karate in a modern way. Were you criticized by your peers in Japan?**

Very much so. Even my own instructor criticized me for using music and giving demonstrations in a park. I was really upset and confused. I kept asking myself if I was doing something wrong. Then my mother, Masu, whom I consider to be the greatest inspiration in my life, came to the United States and saw me perform. That gave me a lot of power and strength. She basically Said that everyone was jealous because of my new position. She told me that people were paying to watch the demonstrations and that I had to give them a great show. The final turning point was at the WUKO World Championships in Long Beach, California, in 1975. I gave a great demonstration in front of all the great masters from Japan, including the President of the WUKO, Mr. Sasakawa. I received a standing ovation, the biggest of the whole tournament. I guess that day they understood that I was not prostituting the art but drawing more attention to it. That's why I didn't understand the initial criticism at all. I really like the feeling of history and respect that the traditional approach provides.

**Sensei, what are shito ryu's strong points?**

The founder, Kenwa Mabuni, studied under two major teachers, Yasutsune Itosu (Shuri-te) and Kanryo Higaonna (Naha-te). He combined the soft and circular approach of Naha with the hard and more linear techniques from the Shuri system. He also added part of Tomari-te, creating a very versatile Karate method. You see, style does not matter; it's the instruction what really counts.

Personally, I prefer not to make comparisons between styles. Each individual merely expresses to the best of their ability their own understanding of a style. It is somehow inappropriate to make public comparisons since they are of such a purely personal nature.

**With all the technical changes during the last decades, do you think there is still "pure" shotokan, shito ryu, et cetera?**

Actually I don't think there ever was any pure Karate system that was passed modified or unchanged. Mabuni Sensei modified and changed what he studied and learnt from his teachers, Funakoshi Sensei did the same thing, Ohtsuka Sensei did the same…it is a normal to do that in the evolution and preservation of the art of Karate. All the teachers adapt and change things according to their own beliefs and perception of things that they pass onto their students. If we keep the system "pure" with no improvements or changes, eventually will be obsolete. It is true that probably nowadays the process of change is way faster than it was before; magazines, DVD, internet, seminars, etc…expose the students to the arts like never before. There is much more information and this information affects the way the teachers see, teach and change their methods and the Martial Arts in general.

I truly think there is a martial art out there to suit everyone, some styles which are very athletic and require a great deal of flexibility, others are hard and physically punishing. There are also gentle and soft styles, ones that mimic animals, competition styles and practical styles. The key is to find the one for you….

**What makes a martial art style special?**

The talent and skill of the practitioner. It's that simple. A good teacher shares his knowledge and experience with the students. Some of the students are capable of becoming masters in the future, others are not. Either they don't have the talent or they don't have the motivation or time. They won't be those who will make the style grow. The future of any style lies on a few talented men who are willing to work, research and develop the basics to a higher level. Of course, the media has a lot of responsibility in deciding which style is the most popular. Certain areas of the Martial Arts can be called a sport, but the Martial Arts are very complex because of the emphasis on tradition, self-defense, and reality usage. The competitive spirit in sports is the opposite of the Martial Arts. We were taught to be humble and not use the art in a

# One-on-One with Fumio Demura

way that shows arrogance. In a combat sport you have to have this quality or you will never get to the next level.

**Do you believe in practicing with training equipment for actual "contact" in the execution of the techniques?**

Yes, I do. Early in my training I became aware of the importance of having solid contact when you are training your "waza" (techniques). This led me to research in the kind of training equipment that was available at that time. Traditionally we used the makiwara but in the United States of America the heavy bag was used by boxers and even in Japan some Karate schools had it there for developing power in the kicking techniques. When you hit a target like a focus mitt, heavy bag, a kicking shield or similar, you get a "feedback" in your technique and muscles. This feedback makes you adjust and accommodate the physical movement to actually hitting a target with power. The muscles in the body must react and contract in a very different way that when you simply execute the technique in the air. Correct technique will give you the necessary speed in the movement but power is a combination of speed and strength. Using a target to hit teaches the muscles how and when to contract properly and how to stabilize the body for the reverberation from the impact. When you see someone with nice technique but poor power levels, you know something is lacking in their training.

**How important is the makiwara training?**

# IN HIS OWN WORDS

It is very important. It strengthens the whole body – the hips, shoulders, wrists, and hands. Hitting the makiwara is essential to a strong punch – not by getting big knuckles, but by developing a tight fist and solid wrist. It also strengthens the stance and helps teach correct ma-ai (fighting distance). While such training doesn't need to be excessive, I find that karateka who use the makiwara have more confidence in their punching and striking ability.

**What is the best way for beginning students to improve?**

Set goals according to each level of your training and practice consistently. Beginners should learn the basics because they need to establish a solid foundation for the more advanced techniques. It is true, though, that many people get bored and discouraged so they start focusing more on different movements and advanced kata instead of working on the basics. This can be more appealing in the beginning but when the years pass by and you face an opponent who has a sound knowledge and skill of the basics, you'll find out that you are lacking something. Even if new techniques and movements appear more appealing, they all are based on the fundamentals and are simply a personal expression.

**What is the most important physical quality?**

Try to be in good shape all the time. Your body is the secret. Keep your body clean and follow a good nutrition plan. Food is the fuel of your body. Be careful what kind of food you eat because it will directly affect the way you

# One-on-One with Fumio Demura

will perform in competition and training. Keep your cardiovascular training up and eat a balanced diet. From the technical point of view, the student should pay attention to the development of the basics. This is paramount. Then he or she needs the right mentality and attitude for the training. Strive to develop yourself as a whole, not only as a fighter but as a complete human being as well.

### Would you recommend the multi-style training approach?

No, not for beginners at least, since this can be very confusing. For advanced level students, I think it is very positive to learn something from other arts; the more you know about something, the more you can appreciate it. It doesn't mean that you have to like everything, but at least understand it and have some respect for it. Mixing Karate' styles is just getting to the same point by choosing a different road. When a person reaches the pinnacle of a specific martial art, they should have reached the pinnacle of all Martial Arts. I would like to think what I teach is usable and effective – that is valuable. I always want people to obtain good value when they come to train with me and to remember what was taught.

### Is any style of martial art better than the rest?

The truth is that if you are happy practicing a particular style, then that is the best style for you. Period. We should respect the fact that people train Martial Arts for different reasons and in the end it is the person who makes the style work. Respect for other styles is very important—even if you don't share the same point of view with their approach to combat you should respect them and not criticize whatever is that they are doing. Without respect there is nothing. Respect is a problem we all face in our lives and the lack if it is dangerously growing in the modern society. Instructors of all styles and systems should strive to preserve the ethics and traditions that the Martial Arts were based on. Knowledge in the Martial Arts does not mean memorizing a technique, but learning why the technique works and its application under very different circumstances.

### Then, what is you opinion about mixing styles in the individual's Martial Arts journey?

Well, one thing is to study different methods of Martial Arts and another is to create or develop your own "way" by mixing styles. Let me explain what I mean by this: if you study aikido and then you use some of the wristlocks and ground control after you do the application of bunkai kata movement, I think this is perfectly fine. You "added" the wristlock knowledge that you absorbed studying aikido to become a more effective karateka in controlling an aggressor on the ground.

A very different thing is to "create" a new system that is a composition of many methods. The different styles have different principles and applications to work and some of them are simply not compatible with each other. If you take the wheels of a pick up truck they won't fit into a Ferrari. It is not as "easy" as it looks on paper. Some people think that Bruce Lee did that, but I can tell you that is not what he was trying to teach his students.

**Do you think traditional kata has to be changed to adapt to modern times?**

Kata movements should not change at all for the sake of "looks". It is the traditional part of Karate. Karate is an art. In the past, it was used for combat and fighting. Perhaps a master – at a certain time - altered part of the kata for certain reasons, according to his combat experience. To me, though, the kata has to be kept intact even in modern times. Training methods and sparring techniques may change, but not kata.

**How important is kata in the overall Karate training?**

Well, the main thing is that practicing a kata without deeply understanding its principles and concepts as they apply to actual combat it is like using a word without knowing its meaning and definition. It is that simple. Kata means many things and can be used in many different ways to improve the practitioners skill and development in Karate. They preserve tradition but the real meaning of these kata seems to have been lost today. The original idea developed by the founder is simply not there anymore.

This is the main problem; if the original essence and meaning of a kata has been lost, how can we actually practice that form without putting the proper emphasis where it belongs? What are we "really" doing when we are doing that kata? We need to know the exact purpose or purposes for which it was intended. Knowing its meaning and where to put the emphasis will give the student the guideline to perform the kata correctly.

**Is it important to involve a partner in the training of bunkai?**

Extremely important! Bunkai is what gives sense to the kata. And bunkai has to be practiced with a partner. Kata only comes to life when you actually

# One-on-One with Fumio Demura

apply the movements against an opponent. Kata regularly is part of the process to improving your kumite. If you practice kata correctly with good visualization and breathing it can become almost like meditation and help you reach a deeper and more meaningful understanding of Karate. Obviously you need to understand and comprehend how these movements should be adjusted to a life attacking opponent…but essentially that is what gives "meaning" to the kata. If you look back, the main reason why the masters developed and created kata was for preserve self-defense techniques and keep basics together for a practice that involved different directions and body changes.

Some of the bunkai is theoretical but a good sensei will be able to choose and adapt many of the techniques for today's self-defense situations. Kata practice is an essential element in learning Karate.

**You often mention that kata should be taught in a certain progression according to the student's level. What do you mean by that?**

Traditionally, a new student didn't learn the Pi Nan or Heian right away. There are the Taikyoku kata, the GekiSai in Goju Ryu, etc. What I mean by learning kata in a progression is similar to a young boy trying to read Albert Camus, or Jean Paul Satre or Immanuel Kant. Yes, he can actual "read" the

# IN HIS OWN WORDS

words but he won't be able of "understand" what these men meant with those words because he simply does not have the depth and knowledge to comprehend and process their ideas. It is the same with kata in Karate. A young12 years old "Suparimpei" or "Chatanyara No Kusanku". These katas are meant to a more mature karateka. Due to the demands of sport competition, nowadays the students learn the movements, they copy all what they can and then use it in a competition. From outside maybe he or she is doing the movements "right" but when you look deeper in their actions you realize that there is a lot missing, that this practitioner has not the understanding of what they are doing. The main problem with that is these students will assume they have a "level" that they simply do not have. A lot of time and attention should be put into the correct kata for each level and years later - little by little - adding more complex and difficult kata to their repertoire. It is alright for young students to want to learn these very advanced kata but the teachers should discourage them to do so because their progress will be jeopardized.

**Do you think YouTube, books and internet has anything to do with that?**

Absolutely! I think books can a great supplement to Martial Arts training, but ultimately, the right way to learn is to have a live instructor to train with.

Traditionally, the old masters when they wrote a book they left moves out…intentionally! If you look in some of the older books out there, you'll see maybe five or six movements missing from a particular kata. So any book needs to be very in-depth and step-by-step in its illustrations and explanations in order to really get the essence of the kata across.

YouTube is pretty good for demonstrating techniques and kata, but unfortunately, a lot of people tend to watch the videos without really absorbing the

# One-on-One with Fumio Demura

techniques through training at the Dojo. You really need to have a solid direct instruction to understand the kata properly. Unfortunately, today we have what some people call…"Sensei YouTube".

**What is the essence of Karate training?**

Although the art of Karate emphasizes individuality as the ultimate ideal, it is impossible to learn the art by oneself, or through a book. Just as a child needs guidance in learning to walk, so too do the novices need instruction in learning how to protect themselves. Only after years of practice can one comprehend the theories of the real art of Karate-do. And only with a proper foundation can one venture out on their own to discover new dimensions in the art by themselves.

**What is your opinion of full contact Karate and kickboxing?**

The emergence of kickboxing within the Karate world in the 70s was inevitable once the development of those skills needed for non-contact Karate tournaments became the dominant aspect of Karate training. There was a need to know if the techniques worked in reality, in a less controlled environment, but of course there was a big problem.

**And that was?**

By wearing boxing gloves, or pads on your hands and feet, you can land the blows, but the effect of the blows are muted and so you eventually end up doing a kind of boxing in long trousers, where you need to throw combinations to finish the opponent. Now proponents of this approach say that it is more realistic, but in the street you would not have time to put on your boxing gloves on, and the attacks to the joints, groin, et cetera were forbidden in Full Contact Karate, so it has its own restrictions. When boxers have got involved in street scuffles they have damaged their hands, so throwing those kinds of techniques in a real fight might not be the best solution. All forms of gloved fighting have rules.

**Do you think the reason people feel attracted to Martial Arts has changed over the years?**

Yes, definitely. The society is different and people's mentality has changed, their goals in life are very different compared to those of forty or fifty years ago. Sometimes those changes are a matter of personal convenience and have nothing to do with the natural change of things. But every change is not necessarily positive and sometimes is advisable for us to throw out the new and bring in the old. I believe everybody has a different reason to start practicing but mostly I think they main reason is for self-defense and health. Today if you want to learn to fight you don't have to spend five years in a Martial Arts school polishing your punches and kicks. This is one of the reasons why people criticize other arts. Let's say I am not interested in fighting but I truly enjoy the physical demands of the training. The art you choose and that makes you happy and the makes you enjoy your training are highly effective in your life, and if you become a better human being, then these are good for you.

### Why is it, in your opinion, that a lot of students start falling away after two or three years of training?

A lack of a real love for the art of Karate and also a lack of patience. Many people today who begin training in the Martial Arts do so as a hobby. In times past, people trained out of a true love of the Martial Arts, or out of a need for self-defense. Today however, many people go out and see a Martial Arts movie and think it would be a fun thing to do. They do not have a deep interest, but see it just as any other recreational activity, so they lose interest quickly. Today, true martial artist are very hard to find.

### In traditional Martial Arts, why is frustration part of the teaching process?

If a student can't survive an injured ego, how is he going to survive the grueling training to come? Frustration is good if both the teacher and the student know how to use it. But frustration is just part of the training. The important thing is to understand it properly and keep training just as before. In fact, the idea of not being discouraged and disappointed are preconceived ideas that we have before getting into the dojo – and fortunately all of them are shattered to pieces on the mat.

### Can weightlifting, running, swimming, et cetera replace training time on the mat?

First of all, I don't think supplementary training will ever compensate for a lack of dojo time. Train Karate first, if it is Karate what you are interested in. Then when you get some extra time, use it for additional training that allows you to improve the physical aspects necessary to excel in the art. Keep in mind that this supplementary training should be very specific for Karate or

# One-on-One with Fumio Demura

you'll be wasting your time. Everything you do must have a purpose or an application to enhance your skills as a Karate practitioner. Remember that there is no substitute for hard dojo training and it is not the quantity of time spent training but rather the quality.

The key is to balance every single element in your training so that one aspect will help the others. You don't want to be unbalanced in Karate. Remember that the secret is balance, not only in Martial Arts but in life as well. To be successful you have to have goals and work in that direction. You have to train hard and smart—otherwise everything you want will just be a dream. A goal is an impossible dream if you don't take the necessary steps to make it happen.

**Do you feel variety is the key to avoid training burn-out?**

I do. Sooner or later your body is going to need a rest. It is then when you can stop and do some other kind of exercise to "move the body in a different way". Swimming is a very good exercise and it can be very important part of the recovery. It's a great cardiovascular workout and relaxes the muscles and doesn't put any stress in your joints, which is a plus. Weight training and Yoga are great and you can do these once in a while.

# IN HIS OWN WORDS

**❝**All the teachers adapt and change things according to their own beliefs and perception of things that they pass onto their students. If we keep the system "pure" with no improvements or changes, eventually will be obsolete.**❞**

# One-on-One with Fumio Demura

**Who would you like to have trained with that you have not (dead or alive) and why?**

One person would be Japanese swordsman Miyamoto Musashi – because he was straightforward, he anticipated the results and the opponent, and simplicity was his expertise.

**How have you stayed so motivated for so long?**

I believe that your own spirituality as an individual has a lot to do with the motivation you need to gain success in life. I'm not necessarily talking from a

religious point of view—I have strong faith in myself and in my spirit. This boosts my confidence in everything I do in life. I always set goals and then work to accomplish them. I have been doing this since I was a kid. Every goal is a project that I have to finish. I take one step at a time and pace myself properly to reach the finish line. I always want to excel in anything I do. But I don't get locked into any particular outcome. You have to be flexible enough to change your goals if circumstances change. Life often takes different directions that you have no control over, and your goals should adapt to your current situation and environment. "Realistic" is the key word here—set realistic goals and then focus on them. Being focused is a very important part of achieving anything. Part of being focused is staying relaxed. This is the only way you can keep yourself focused and motivated for long periods of time.

**What are the most important points in your teaching methods?**

The important points to teaching Karate and Martial Arts in general is to get the student to trust the structure of the technique, and not depend too much on muscular strength to overcome the opponent. We must also teach students to be patient. Everything in nature has its timing. When we plant a seed, we water it, nurture it and give it sunlight. Eventually it begins to grow. If when we see the plant growing, if we begin pulling on it, in order to help it grow, we will only kill it. The same is true with Karate. It takes time for skill to develop. We simply cannot rush the process. We must let the natural learning process take place.

### What is your role as a teacher?

I see myself as a guide. I am just a tool for my students to develop themselves. It's important to know how to teach and share knowledge according to the student's needs and abilities. These days many people think only about fighting. Fighting is something natural for the human being and learning how to use your skills in combat is part of traditional Bujutsu and Budo. But it's important to also teach how to avoid fighting.

In a way, by learning how to fight we also learn the value of not fighting. Self-control is very important. Martial Arts training gives you a feeling of safety. No ones trains in order to attack someone or to pick on others. Training forms good reflexes and presents one with a moral code for life. Such training makes us all better human beings. I would also strongly advise not to intellectualize the arts. Karate and Martial Arts in general can be intellectualized but the real practice is what is important. It takes more patience and hard work and less words.

### How much is the teacher responsible of the student's acts?

Definitely the teacher should set a good example for the students to follow but he can't be responsible of the student's behavior outside the dojo, especially if these students are grown men and women. The teacher can act like an advisor to the adult student but he can't force the students to do or behave in a certain way. Nobody is perfect and the teacher should focus on helping the students to overcome their difficulties and move through life in an honorable way. His job is to make the student a better person.

### When do you know when to fight and when to step back in a real situation?

You should always avoid the fight. Do not look for it and try to avoid the fight at all cost. This is what I teach to my students. Sometimes, there are critical situations when there is no other way out and we need to fight. We need to fight when we are truly in danger in a situation where any other solution is not possible.

It is important that as true martial artists we strive to stay away from any physical confrontation that involves hurting any other human being.

# One-on-One with Fumio Demura

If you are provoked you analyze the situation and if there is no true danger for you then you simply stay calm and back off, but if you see that you can't avoid the fight, then try to defeat your aggressor.

I like to quote of a wonderful little paragraph called "The Peaceful Warrior,": Once, while training in the Chinese sword, I asked my teacher why, if I was striving to be inwardly calm and at peace, did I need to learn the ways of a warrior? "Would it not be more tranquil and serene to be a gardener and tend the plants?" I asked. "Tending the garden," my master replied, "is a relaxing pastime, but it does not prepare one for the inevitable battles of life. It is easy to be calm in a serene setting. To be calm and centered when under attack is much more difficult. So, therefore, I tell you that "it is far better to be a warrior tending his garden, rather than a gardener making war."

The point is that you do not always get to choose when you may be attacked with violence, so you need to be ready at all times.

**Do you feel there are any fundamental differences between karateka from different countries?**

Yes, there are substantial differences but this is normal. The cultural background is different therefore the mentality, the education, the way each group perceives life is different. Japan culture is very geared toward the arts of Budo, the traditional Japanese values are part of the arts too. This doesn't happen in any other country because of their history and background.

It is up to the Japanese instructor to "teach" the Budo values at the same time he teaches the physical art. He needs to know how to progressively incorporate these traditional Budo values into the mentality and life of the students. Some will be willing to learn and apply these principles to their lives and

# IN HIS OWN WORDS

some other won't. Budo in Japan is a philosophy, a tradition, a kind of religious belief. In other countries, they have their own set of beliefs and these must be respected.

**And what about the physical differences?**

The body types are different. But I have to say that this is changing too. We had the idea of Westerners being taller and thinner than their Japanese counterpart. Well, look at the Japanese competitors today.... they are tall, long limbs, pretty much like the competitor from the rest of the world. It is true that some genetics are involved. The Japanese tradition of sitting in "seiza" since we are kids develops

the hips and the flexibility in the ankles while in the Western world this tradition doesn't exist. Eventually this can make a difference but not so much that one person cannot be an excellent karateka and athlete if he or she decides to compete at international level.

**Talking about physical differences...do you change the way you teach depending of the gender? Do you teach a woman different from the way you teach a man?**

This is a very interesting question. I do not alter or modify the fundamental training of Karate. Karate is Karate and I teach the techniques regardless of the gender of the student. Both women and men are interesting in the art and the sport so I share these with them without any difference. When I alter things is when I teach self-defense. Women have to use the body in a different way a man should during a physical altercation. A man can punch and be effective but it is harder for a woman to use the same type of techniques when she has to protect herself. The targets she aims for should be different too. A female should use finger jabs, strikes to the groin and focus on soft areas. It is in the aspect of self-defense and the self-preservation mentality when I teach different. Other than that, Karate is Karate.

# One-on-One with Fumio Demura

### How do you perceive the modern and competitive approach to the art of Karate?

I think that people want too much too quickly. They want to run before knowing how to walk and learn advanced techniques without mastering the basics. You can't have a strong house without a strong foundation. The stronger the basics, the stronger the house – it's as simple as that. Unfortunately, a lot of practitioners don't understand this principle. Competition has good and bad sides. The worst thing is losing sight of your training just to win a trophy. Sometimes, the trophy gets to be the most important thing, and that's not right. The student loses so much when they think like that.

On the other hand, the good part is that competition can help the student learn about goal-setting. This allows the student to go through a learning process that includes a viable system of performance grading at the end of the process. I know that the end doesn't always seem to work, but what is important is that the students went through the process by increasing their training, focused their minds, et cetera. I would like to see all Karate practitioners understand that competition is just a small aspect of their total training – it is not the ultimate aim.

A lot of people who practice Martial Arts can't distinguish the differences between true and phony Karate. It is impossible for any instructor to try to educate everybody. Therefore, it is very important that Karate practitioners research and educate themselves about the art they practice. Also, many karate-ka get lost in the beauty of the forms (kata) and forget about the final objective of every single Karate technique, which is efficiency. A kata, no matter how fancy or beautiful it looks, has fundamental components that can abs should be used for many purposes, like physical conditioning, self-defense, health, etc. The ability to execute the techniques of Karate correctly must be combined with the power to damage an opponent when necessary.

I agree with the fact that Karate is a great art and a wonderful sport for entertaining, but to sacrifice the richness of a great art for its gymnastics is like trading a diamond for a piece of broken glass.

### Is there anything that you dislike most about the Martial Arts as practiced and taught today?

The lack of respect for others. I believe that this is only a reflection of what is going on in today' society in general. However, I feel that it is the responsibility of Martial Arts teachers to be positive role models and to set a good example for their students.

# IN HIS OWN WORDS

### Is it important to specialize in a few techniques or have a wide repertoire?

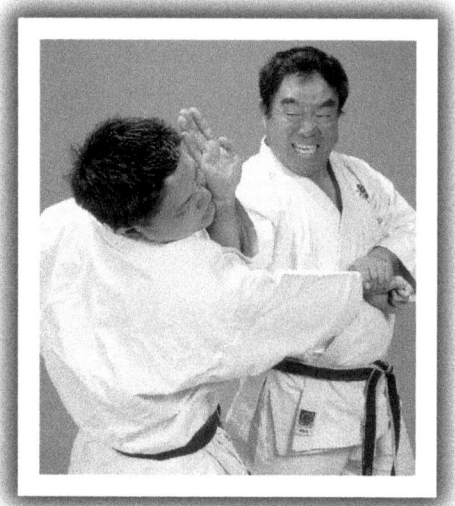

Everything boils down to what you are looking for in your Karate training. If you decide to compete then you need to have a wide understanding of many techniques, although not necessarily to use them all. You need to know them and understand the way they work so you can counter them with your specialties—that is the key. You may have three or four special moves, but it doesn't mean these few techniques are the only thing you know. However, you must know many different ways of using your special moves or pretty soon all your opponents will know how to stop you before you even think about trying. You need to have a variety of tactical ways to apply your techniques in order to keep your opponent guessing what's going to happen next.

### As a Karate and Kobudo teacher, do you feel both arts are related?

Of course they are. I always say that they are like the two wheels of a bicycle. They work under the same principles. A full study of Kobudo is not for everyone, but I strongly recommend some weapons training to everyone. My approach to Kobudo is different from that of my instructors, though; in the beginning I use it more for supplemental training.

### What do you consider to be the best Kobudo weapon?

I don't think there is a "best" weapon. Each weapon helps you to develop different things. In fact, the Kobudo weaponry is divided into three different categories: long weapons like the bo; short weapons like the kama, Sai, and Tonfa; and hiding weapons such as the Nunchaku.

### But you always felt very comfortable with the Nunchaku?

Yes. I consider the Nunchaku to be a very good weapon. Unfortunately, a lot of people misunderstand its use – maybe because of Bruce Lee's movies. They

# One-on-One with Fumio Demura

think you really need that much movement and swinging, when in real life situations one simple swing is all it takes. There is no traditional kata in Nunchaku training, but old masters made their own forms for practice and to structure the techniques – which I feel is very acceptable and important.

**Sensei, please tell us about the main Kobudo weapons. Let's start with the "Bo".**

The real origin of the Bo, Kon, or straight staff is sill obscure in the Kobudo history. The Okinawans had to rely on farming instruments to protect themselves since the inhabitants of the island were barred from owning any sort of weapons, and it is believed that this weapon was developed from the Tenbin, a staff held across the shoulder that was used to carry buckets hanging from each end with water or food. When attacked, the farmer would drops these and use the staff for self-protection.

The size and dimensions of the Bo will vary depending on the practitioner but the regular Bo is about six feet long or as described in Japanese roku shaku-bo. There also are other lengths and shapes for the Bo, like the four-foot (yon shaku-bo) and the nine-foot (kyu shaku-bo). As far as the shape is concerned, some traditional teachers still use the square and hexagonal shape because these multiple edges provide a more destructive effect. Some of the most common circularly shaped types of Bo are:

1. Maru-bo (round)
2. Kaku-bo (four-sided)
3. Rokkaku-bo (eight-sided) and,
4. Take-bo (bamboo).

The thickness also varies due to personal preferences, but it typically measures 1¼-inch thick at the center (Chukon-bu) and around 3/4-inch at the end (Kontei). This difference in thickness facilitates strong and powerful whipping actions and guarantees that the Bo's fulcrum stays at its center as rigidity is simultaneously reduced, which helps easy handling.

To determine if the Bo possesses the correct shape and handling qualities, we can simply roll it across a flat surface; if it is properly constructed, it will roll smoothly. If it is bent or warped, the weapon will roll unevenly, making a loud clatter. Modern Bo manufacturers use strong wood like red or white oak to produce the weapon. These have replaced the old bamboo and increased the sturdiness of the weapon.

There are four basic holds when practicing with the Bo. You should develop a familiarity with all of them so you can switch holds at will and at high speed

# IN HIS OWN WORDS

when performing kata and sparring combinations. Almost all Bo-jutsu actions [both single and complex] are executed by grabbing the weapon with the basics grips. These are:

**a.** Jun Nigiri (Basic Hold)
**b.** Gyaku Nigiri (Reverse Hold)
**c.** Hasami Nigiri (Palm Hold)
**d.** Yose Nigiri (Double Hold)

Remember, no matter how proficient you may be using the Bo, your technique will never be perfect because perfection is something unattainable in the Martial Arts. It is a goal we all must strive for but that we'll never achieve.

## What about the "Sai"?

The Sai is one of the most popular weapons in the art of Kobudo. Its shape and unique versatility offers a great training challenge for any dedicated practitioner. Originally, the Sai was used to drag the soil by one farmer, while another would plant the seed. The farmer, when attacked by the Samurai, would use this tool to protect himself against the sword. It was normal for a farmer to carry even three Sai with him. This was based on the fact that sometimes the farmer could actually throw one Sai toward his opponent. This surprise action was the key for victory in many encounters. The third Sai usually was carried in the belt.

In the beginning, the tip of the Sai was sharp and only lately has been blunted and rounded for training purposes. Its techniques are very dangerous, and a thrust to the neck or the face can be lethal in a real fight. Since it is no longer used as a real weapon for combat, the material has changed and now we can find great steel and chromed-plated Sai in many Martial Arts stores around the world.

# One-on-One with Fumio Demura

❝You should always avoid the fight. Do not look for it and try to avoid the fight at all cost. This is what I teach to my students.❞

# IN HIS OWN WORDS

The Sai is formed of two important parts, the curved prong and the main stem. When this weapon was introduced to Japan it was called "Jutte" and it bore a single prong at the handle. Japanese police found this weapon to be very effective in controlling aggressors and they started to use it more and more.

In many ways, the techniques used in Sai training are very similar to the movements used in Karate. They follow similar principles and they require a sense of "kime" like the empty hand actions. One important point that the practitioner should develop in training with the Sai is dexterity in the fingers. The fast change of grasps and different gripping methods require from the practitioner a high level of proficiency in maneuvering the weapon. This is the reason why, usually, no beginners are taught the use of the Sai.

The complete anatomy of the Sai involves seven parts:

1. The point.
2. The blade.
3. The prongs.
4. The guard.
5. The guard center.
6. The handle.
7. The butt.

All these parts have a function in the use of the weapon, and in order to give the user a better grip, the handle usually is wrapped with a cotton ribbon for a more secure grab.

The gripping of the weapon is very simple when compared to other tools; the Sai can be held in only two ways: pointing the tip outward or pointing the tip inward. These two methods will dictate what kind of flipping action we are going to do with the weapon. The flipping action is a very important movement when training, and the wrist and elbow should be properly conditioned to precisely execute the snapping movement of the technique. Try to relax and don't try to put too much body weight when you snap the Sai; the secret for the right snap is speed and control. Any additional tension on your shoulders will decrease the power in the technique. It is important that we correctly train to develop the right feeling of a whipping motion when using the Sai. These flipping motions have no real counterpart in empty hand Karate; therefore, they must be learned separately. Never forget that good technique stems from good form. The ideal technique is always perfect in form and

# One-on-One with Fumio Demura

places you in the best position for the next movement in combat.

### Tonfa...

The Tonfa originally was a wooden handle fitted into a hole on the side of a millstone used by the Okinawans for milling grain. This handle became a very effective weapon for self-protection. The main part of the Tonfa is a large hardwood body about 15–20 inches in length, with a cylindrical grip secured to the main body about six inches from one end.

Karate and Kobudo are mutually supported arts and many of the Tonfa actions reflect principles used in Karate. The practice of any Kobudo weapon improves coordination, strength, and balance for the Karate practitioner.

The Tonfa is a great training tool by itself. It develops strong hands, wrists, and forearms, since all the actions are generated using these parts of the human body. For instance, the snapping action of the Tonfa originated in the wrist is similar to the wrist action of a Karate punch. In many ways, training with this weapon will increase the karateka's empty hand skills in a very short time.

The correct length of the Tonfa is determined from the grip to the back head, and the back head should extend past the elbow by one-half inch. Once this important distance is determined, we can adjust the balance of the weapon by reducing the length from the grip to the front head. Based on these requirements, every practitioner should choose a length and balance to fit his/her personal characteristics. Although the basic configuration of the weapon is the same, the main body of the Tonfa can have different shapes.

Two of the most popular materials for Tonfa manufacturing are oak and cherry wood. Many people like their Tonfa varnished for better look, but if

# IN HIS OWN WORDS

you are using it for practical combat techniques and training, this varnish soon will go away. No matter what, remember to clean it periodically with a cloth moistened with olive or other vegetable oil.

The Tonfa is composed of seven parts:

1. Front head.
2. Grip.
3. Grip head.
4. Top of main body.
5. Bottom of main body.
6. Side of main body.
7. Back head.

The basic grip of the Tonfa is very similar to the Karate fist and is firm enough so the weapon doesn't drop while in use. Due to the twisting and snapping actions, the grip has to be very relaxed but firm enough to apply power at the moment of impact by squeezing and tightening up the fingers. This is the reason why, in order to be effective using this weapon, the practitioner must develop strong wrists. The key for a powerful swing of the Tonfa is to minimally bend the elbow when you are swinging the weapon. Always keep the arms extended when rotating the Tonfa.

The blocking actions resemble those used in Karate and the principles are almost identical. The attacking maneuvers are varied and they can be more complex when we use two Tonfa at the same time. Always remember that an effective performance and use of the Tonfa involves three different principles: maai, kime, and mushin, and perfect synchronized action of the hands, elbows, and hips.

**And finally the Nunchaku.**

My good friend and Martial Arts icon, Bruce Lee, was responsible for bringing the

# One-on-One with Fumio Demura

Nunchaku into the spotlight. He used it in his movies as a new "attraction" for the viewers, and his skills were second to none. Although popularized by Bruce Lee, the forerunner of the Nunchaku was an instrument used as a bit for horses; it was not used as a weapon until later on when Okinawan farmers converted farm implements into protective devices. This weapon was constructed of two hardwood sticks connected by a rope braided from horses' tails. Because of its simple appearance, the Nunchaku easily was mistaken for a harmless bundle of two sticks. The Okinawan karateka saw the efficiency of this tool as a protective weapon and immediately incorporated into their arsenal.

The length of the Nunchaku should equal the distance from the middle of the hand to the elbow, but it also should be adjusted to fit the practitioner's height and arm power. The weapon is divided into seven different parts:

1. The rope/chain (Himo or Kusari).
2. Top (Kontoh).
3. Hole (Ana).
4. Upper Area (Jokon).
5. Middle Area (Chukon).
6. Lower Area (Kikon).
7. Botom Area (Kontei).

Every part of the Nunchaku can be used as a weapon and has a certain utility. For instance, the bottom and top can be used to jab or spear, the middle area is used to block and control in close-quarter range, and the rope or chain is very practical to pinch or choke the opponent.

When analyzing the different designs of the weapon, we will find out that there are many different "shapes" used for the Nunchaku. The main categories are: a) Maru-gata (Round); b) Hakakukei (Octagonal); c) So-setsu-kon (Long and Short); d) Han-kei (Half-size); e) San-setsu-kon (Three Piece Nunchaku); and f) Yon-setsu-kon (Four Piece).

The grasping methods are simple but they require diligent training and practice. The weapon can be grasped at the bottom, the middle area, and the top, and these grasping methods can be combined and altered on both sides, which gives us several possibilities of maneuvering the Nunchaku. The possibility of changing grasps and gripping methods during the action provides this weapon with great versatility and a high degree of deception for our opponent. Although the basic grasping-change action involves two hands, it is the true mark of a master to change grips with one hand while using the Nunchaku to attack or defend.

# IN HIS OWN WORDS

**❝Karate-do teaches us how to concentrate and how to bring the body and the mind together.❞**

# One-on-One with Fumio Demura

Due to its nature, the Nunchaku is mainly a swinging weapon and this dictates the type of defensive and attacking actions that we can do in combat. The "snapping" techniques allow for a faster recovery to the on-guard position but the swinging actions are more difficult to control specially after hitting the target. Constant practice should be allocated in the training time to learn how to recover the weapon; the idea is to hit the target and recover the weapon safely so we can use it again. The recovery action is the most important technique for a Kobudo practitioner when using this weapon.

We can state that all the techniques developed for the use of Nunchaku are self-defense oriented. Please do not mistake the "flashy" and "attractive" swinging actions that you can see in movies and TV with the "real" use of this weapon for self-protection. Once you understand the use and essential principles of the Nunchaku, you will be able of developing a limitless amount of efficient and practical techniques.

You've have been involved in the movie industry, working with celebrities such as Sean Connery, Burt Lancaster, Wesley Snipes, and many more. But you received the majority of your recognition for your work in "The Karate Kid".

I've been very fortunate. But, as result of all that work, and seminars and videos, I had a heart attack. That situation forced me take a look at my lifestyle. I used to leave the dojo for long periods of time to travel, but now I try to focus more on school and doing a little bit of movie work. That's it, and I'm happy. I like to help people. Sometimes people think that I'm doing great things for others, but in fact that's what a martial artist is supposed to be doing – helping others. That's what Martial Arts are all about.

**What is your personal training like now?**

I guess everybody goes through the same process. When we are young, we try to show how tough we are and we do a lot of kumite. When we get older and our bodies start to hurt, then we start to appreciate kata training much more. I emphasize more kata and kihon in my personal training. Sensei Sakagami always told me that the original Okinawan kata were easier on the body, because they put less stress on the joints. I didn't appreciate the truth of this until years later. The learning process in art of Karate-do never ends. Your knowledge in the art depends on how much research you do to understand the application of the style to different situations and fighting methods. For me, I definitely feel there is more to learn about Karate-do.

# IN HIS OWN WORDS

### How important is an open mind in a Karate practitioner?

Extremely important. Sometimes it has more to do with being free from a strong [and most likely "toxic" influence] rather that just being open minded.

### How much of Japanese culture can be found in the art of Karate?

Karate is a product of the Japanese culture, and if the practitioner has some grasp of the Japanese philosophy, culture, art, etc., it can help the overall understanding of Karate. But, under no circumstance, can these elements substitute for actual training and physical practice. Karate-do teaches us how to concentrate and how to bring the body and the mind together. I think that many people today understand about Martial Arts but few people among the practitioners truly understand the real meaning of training. Our training is not there to play out our own fantasies. It has to do with your own life. That is why a true Budo man lives his life in an impeccable way.

### How does mental maturity affect the student's progression in the art?

Some students are gifted and very clever. They progress fast because their bodies allow them to do so, and they begin to practice advanced techniques and forms that are not at their level of maturity in the art. Physically, they can do them but their understanding is not "there" yet. When we talk about building a foundation in Karate, it is not only physically. It implies a mental "foundation," too, and this one comes with time and patience. As instructors, we must be sure that the student follows a natural progression in order to achieve his or her complete potential.

My advice to students is to spend more time on the basic techniques and kata instead of diversifying your training into an endless number of fancy techniques and kata that will bring you momentary recognition. You'll be able to display more techniques than other practitioners of your same rank, but the consequence after years of training will be that you become incapable of developing a more mature and stronger Karate, simply because you never spent the necessary time developing the basics. No basics, no nothing. It's that simple. I want the students to achieve some level of success in their life. There are many different ways to do this. I have used Martial Arts to achieve the kind of success and accomplishments I have. People can learn to take the process they learn at the dojo – setting goals, training hard, being persistent – and apply it to their life outside the dojo.

# One-on-One with Fumio Demura

**Is a black belt or a champion automatically a good teacher?**

A black belt can teach anyone they want, of course, but it doesn't necessarily mean they know how to properly do it. I have seen black belts who have won major championships who cannot properly explain the most basic techniques to a student. They are great as competitors but their ability to communicate is not adequate enough for them to teach properly. The main point is to have the ability to transmit the essence of the art. In the future, they will be the

ones training the students because they can pass the knowledge to future generations. Being a good competitor does not necessarily mean you'll be a good teacher. A good teacher will always know how to help the students recognize and deal with the important points of any technique. Effective teaching is the final responsibility of each instructor.

**How do you see the transition from being a champion or great athlete and competitor to be a teacher?**

Well, there is definitely a big difference being a champion and being a teacher. That transition is something that the practitioner should think about before retiring from competition. A teacher is a person that has the power and influence in changing people's lives. It is not about "him" or "her" anymore. It is about the students. It is the teacher's responsibility to give the student's that push to deal with their lives, to develop self-confidence for anything that they take in life.

Unfortunately being a good competitor or a good fighter doesn't mean that you will be a good teacher, although many people assume so. You should be able of transferring that competition and fighting experience to your students in a way that they can absorb and use. Most of the students are not going to

# IN HIS OWN WORDS

compete so "that" knowledge and experience that the teacher accumulated during is athletic years has to be "adapted" in order to be useful to the students. If they can't do this, they will fall in the trap of trying that the student make the things the way they used to do them and this is a failure from a teacher's perspective.

**What about those that were not champions or very good in competition, can they become good teachers?**

It is also possible that one that a good and dedicated Karate may not have the talent to be a sport Karate champion but he or she has the ability to communicate correctly and connect with the students in a very special way. That is a gift. To be a good teacher you need to understand the details of the technique, how to communicate it properly, make it work for the student – and each student is different, and you have to fully understand how all the things work. Prestige and fame as a champion has nothing to do with the ability to share the art of Karate inside the dojo.

It is hard for a champion to "switch" to teaching mode while he or she is still competing. Competition is all about "you" and teaching is all about the "others", the students. The goal of a good teacher is to make the art work for the students and eventually, make these students better than yourself.

**Some people believe going to Japan to train is highly necessary. Do you share this point of view?**

Who I am and where I come from is not important. Who I learned from is not important. The most important thing is whether what I have learned is practical and it is real. I think that it is important to go to Japan to get a feeling for the culture, the environment, the tradition, etc…but for the physical technique alone it is not necessary at all. There are many top teachers outside of Japan that teach the art in the right way. In short, I would recommend to travel to Japan to have a great experience of the culture and history of Karate,

# One-on-One with Fumio Demura

for the "feeling" of it but not really relevant to learn the technique.

## What are the philosophical teachings behind the study of Karate?

When you learn the art of Karate or any other martial art for that matter, you are learning fighting techniques but this is not a reason to bully others and to be arrogant about it. Budo and Karate training should be used to build your confidence of dealing with a physical altercation. It is this confidence that eventually will defeat the bullies. I believe that a true traditional Karate-do instructor should teach his students the true morality of Martial Arts and a sense of knightliness that should be felt in everything he does.

## What is your overall philosophy of training?

You can train a martial art, or a combat sport, such as Karate, for sportive uses. But while you're doing this, you always have to think about reality. You have to train the sportive methods, but then always keep adapting them and yourself to be able to use them in real situations. You can't lose sight of that or you lose sight of the true art of Karate itself.

Any true martial artist knows that his training is a lifetime endeavor. And there are no short-cuts. After many years of training you achieve what we can call the 'enlightenment of movement' which is simply when the practitioner can visualize the combat value of a movement or posture.

Unfortunately, most of the people are not able of training eight hours a day so we have to try to find a balance so we can incorporate the valuable training we receive into our daily lives.

## Do you feel that you still have further to go in your studies?

Of course! As we get older, our body changes. Sometimes in life we have to face problems. I am not close to what I was physically many years ago but the Budo way is not only related to the physical aspects of the arts. The study of Karate-do involves many different aspects and I still feel that I have room to get better at things....our understanding evolves and our perception of the art also changes with time and depending how we evolver and grow as human beings. Therefore, yes...I think that I still have to go further in the Budo journey.

## What are the requirements for being an instructor and what advice would you give to all Karate instructors?

# IN HIS OWN WORDS

Of course the technical aspect is paramount, but the ability to teach is a very important aspect and some people forget this. Therefore, being an instructor is not an easy task. As a teacher you have to understand the student's goals and mentality and help him to achieve the former and strengthen the latter. The teaching ability to transmit and communicate with the practitioner is paramount in the educational process. Being a good practitioner or exponent in the art of Karate-do is very different from being a good teacher or instructor. You can be one but not the other.

It is important that we focus our attention to take whatever steps are necessary to elevate the level of Karate and Martial Arts in general in the world. We must pass our inheritance to the future generations. I think this is one important aspect of the ancient teachings; they have stood the test of time and are important to our lives and essential to our society.

Train hard and train smart. Don't forget that every aspect of preparation is important and that includes the physical training, the diet and nutrition, the rest, the psychological. Always be a gentleman, regardless if you win or lose in a competition. Don't forget that your opponent is the one who brings the best out of you. For that very reason, he deserves respect. Be gracious at all times, be honest with yourself and chase your dreams because your time is limited.

**You are a very traditional Karate instructor but your demonstrations always show movement and techniques from other arts. Why is that?**

A martial artist should not impose limitations and boundaries when it comes to improve his skill and understanding of combat. I have studied other methods but I do not "mix" them with Karate. I didn't "repackage" my original Karate but I use throws from Judo, wristlocks from Aikido, etc. Why? Because they simply "fit" and "flow" in the technique I am doing at a given time.

**How the art of Karate influenced your life?**

Karate definitely gave me a new direction in life. I had other goals, but my training helped to focus on the aspects that were important in my life. Don't get me wrong, I don't mean that Martial Arts will change your life if you have a basic lack of common sense because they won't. Martial Arts are a great tool if you know how to use the different mental and philosophical aspects for self- improvement. Enrolling in a Karate dojo was the best thing I ever did.

# One-on-One with Fumio Demura

**"Karate students should remember the little victories that Martial Arts have already helped them achieve. Emphasize the positive and it will help you to move on to your next goal. Never give up!"**

# IN HIS OWN WORDS

I truly love the Martial Arts, so for me to keep training and teaching does not require a big effort. I'm blessed because I am doing what I love, so I consider myself a lucky person. I meet a lot of nice people, and many have become my personal friends who I share my life with them. I guess you need motivation when you perform a task you don't enjoy, but when you love what you do and you have fun at it, then motivation is easy. Martial Arts are a great way of life. They give me a peace of mind that helps to balance the rest of my life.

### What is the place of Martial Arts training in our modern society?

Martial Arts training should bring people together but unfortunately you see practitioner being "separated" by their "loyalty' to their styles. In the art of Karate-do you have different styles and then the practitioners distance themselves from the practitioners from other styles. Instead of looking to what other style is doing and how they approach combat, they completely "cancel" other arts without understanding that there is only one "Karate-do". The styles are the personal interpretation of a combat art by the old masters…like the accent of someone speaking Spanish from Spain compared to some speaking Spanish from Argentina. It is not "really" different. We must try to look for the things and aspects that bring all Karate styles together instead of paying attention at the little differences that in the long run are irrelevant.

### How important is Zen in the art of Karate?

A lot of people think of Zen training is like something that has nothing to do with our daily lives or something that is a completely separate thing. To really understand spiritual training, it is important to see it in our daily lives…from moment to moment. Zen must be used to be a compass in our lives…and that compass must point in the right direction. Spiritual training comes from the most unexpected places in life; we need to be aware of things or we are most likely to miss it.

# One-on-One with Fumio Demura

**Do you think Zen and Karate go together?**

This is an interesting question. From a Budo and traditional perspective all Budo systems have some kind of influence from Zen at a high level of practice. From Karate, Judo, Aikido, Kendo, Iaido to the more traditional Jujutsu. In the Japanese culture it is very hard to not find Zen in the arts of Budo. Now, when we look at the current society in Japan, we see more similarities with the Western world. For instance in the Universities they practice Karate and judo but their approach is pure sport so the more philosophical and spiritual aspects of the traditional arts is simply "not there".

In the Western world many people practice Karate as a physical activity and their spiritual journey is fulfilled with their religion or beliefs, therefore they are not interested in Zen.

But for the Japanese Zen and the arts of Budo they go hand in hand in many ways. Let's not forget that the old Samurai studied Zen in order to be mentally prepare for the battle. This is important to remember.

**Throughout the years, have you ever thought about studying other martial art method like Kung Fu, Tae Kwon Do, etc?**

I have been exposed to many systems and I have many great friends who are masters in their own styles. They have shared their knowledge with me and I highly value their skills. This has helped me to better understand other Martial Arts and how they approach combat. It is interesting that having a better understanding of others styles makes you understand better the system that you practice. It makes you look at your "own house" with a different rational.

**Do you feel that all Karate masters should use the same teaching methods?**

Absolutely not… because each karateka is different. A lot of people complain about the way they were trained but never change the methods when they become teachers. For example, if they had been hurt and treated harshly as junior grades, their students were made to suffer in the same way, with the same results – lots of empty space in the dojo. Why continue a negative practice? If something disturbs me, I will change it.

**Do you emphasize competition in your classes?**

Not necessarily. There are very good things about competition and some very bad things, too. Our training is typically about 90 percent towards the traditional dojo training. If a student wishes to compete, then we will alter the training slightly to include the competition aspect. The worst thing about competition is that the student sometimes concentrates too much on the trophy and loses sight of the spirit of Karate. The best thing is competition can help the student learn about goal setting.

Whether you win or lose in a competition. You gain some kind of experience and self-understanding of how you handle unfamiliar situations. It is a great environment to learn from your mistakes.

I can see that, as a martial artist, once you have developed your skills to a certain level you want to test yourself in a competition, but just make sure you do it in a positive way.

### Has sport competition affected the way the art is evolving?

Yes. Competition has affected the way many practitioners train Karate today, and the perception of the outside world is that Karate is simply competition due to the way most instructors teach it. The sportive aspects today are an important part of the whole art—a part where the best compete against the best and raise the technical level of the art. My advice to those who teach traditional Karate-do, however, is that they should incorporate more classes for those people who are not athletes. There are many people out there who don't have the physical attributes of these athletes—people who are normal citizens, who go to work, have family lives and who would like to learn the art for fun and exercise. Teachers should incorporate more classes into their schools and dojo where the training is more relaxed and more natural—where the emphasis relies on learning proper basic techniques and the physical demands are not like those for people who are going to compete.

The art of Karate-do has to be accessible to the regular individual, and progressively bring these people into a more demanding kind of training. The classes should be separated. You cannot have in the same people who will compete in the national championships, training with people who simply want to learn Karate for personal fun and enjoyment. I would like to see more classes where the true essence of Karate-do is being taught. This is what will allow Karate to attract the general public. Otherwise, the art will die out and fewer and fewer students will come to train.

Competition classes and training for athletes who are going to compete should be addressed outside the normal classes. It is something specifically for those individual who spend a lot of time in Karate. These people should be

# One-on-One with Fumio Demura

trained differently. Not everybody should receive competition training. Many people are not interested in competition, but they are interested in receiving the benefits that traditional Karate can bring into their lives.

Tournaments help to develop some of these qualities and have their place in the Martial Arts. I set up my tournaments to have value, not to find out who the best fighter is in the world. My concept of a tournament is training. Tournaments are drills to find the relationship between distance, timing, and speed.

### How important is the diet in the life of a martial artist?

We must understand that a weak body is not suitable for combat. Nutrition is very important since it feeds the body and the body is our tool for the art. I have come to realize that what we put in our bodies is extremely important and I recommend to all martial artists and public in general to be aware of what the eat and what they put in their bodies. Once your body shuts down, there is no turning back. Be aware and be careful of the food you eat. It is your life.

### What should a student look for in a school?

Students should be dedicated and loyal to their teacher and not jump from one instructor to another for no reason. They should be honest with themselves and keep training hard regardless of what their goal may be. Before starting to train under any given instructor, check his credentials and find a little about him. Check a class and see if what he is teaching is what you want to practice and train. Many instructors put too much emphasis on one aspect and forget others—too much competition, too much fitness, or maybe too much self-defense. The teacher should have a balanced approach to the art of Karate-do and not teach only one aspect. There are also differences depending on the country. For instance, in the United States, 90% of the students are interested in self-defense and exercise. Your approach to teaching should

# IN HIS OWN WORDS

be different then. Karate is Karate but it should accommodate the culture of the country where the instructor teaches. That is what I did when I came to the United States.

### What makes a martial art style special?

The talent and skill of the practitioners. It's that simple. A good teacher shares his knowledge and experience with the students. Some of them are capable of becoming masters in the future, others are not. Either they don't have the talent or they don't have the motivation. They won't be those who will make the style grow. The future of the style lies on a few talented men who are willing to work, research and develop the basics to a higher level. Of course, the media has a lot of responsibility in deciding which style is the most popular. Movies have their weight, too, in deciding the most popular style. Remember the Ninja craze? Movies made that happen and then the magazines supported it. It has nothing to do with the techniques or approach of the specific martial art style, it has to do with several external factors impossible for the average Martial Arts instructor and student to control.

### You mentioned once that people sometimes set goals they can't achieve and this is not good. Why is that?

We all have to be realistic about our own potential and abilities. We need to know our limitations so we can excel. Maybe a student doesn't have the potential to be a world champion — very few do. So the teacher needs to motivate the student and get the best out of him without making him believe impossible things. He needs to help the students see their potential without creating false expectations. The same thing goes the other way, too. Teachers who constantly run students down is also bad. Be positive but be realistic. There is a big responsibility on the Sensei's shoulders in this regard.

# One-on-One with Fumio Demura

Sometimes we spend too much time philosophizing over techniques. Using the body and mind in practical training will answer our questions. 'Silence is golden' the old masters used to say.

**Do you think it is necessary to engage in free-fighting to achieve good fighting skills in the street?**

You need to engage in some kind sparring to develop certain physical attributes that will help your ability to protect yourself in the street. It is necessary to get the "feeling" for an "alive" aggression or attack. But let me explain a very important point when trying to transfer sparring or kumite skill to a real self-defense situation. The key is in the mental state. Every attack from the opponent in sparring/kumite has to be "perceived" as a real attack and respond with the same mindset that you would have if you are trying to "survive" in the street. If you spar like it is a game of points, and you are not concern about doing your defensive move first, you will fall into the trap of thinking that because you can score points you can protect yourself in the street and this is nothing further from the truth. Real self-defense does not resemble what we see in sport competition. Competition is an artificial environment created for sport and fun. Sometimes I think it is good to use some kind of protection for allowing certain techniques to be used in kumite.

Another important point is that simply practicing sparring against one opponent is not enough; it is important that you learn how to face two or three opponents at once in order to get a realistic feeling and understanding what is an street situation.

Karate always has been regarded as "ikken-hisatsu" art, that is "killing with one strike." However, people with experience in real combats know how difficult it is to overcome your adversary with one punch or kick. What is your take on this?

In Karate we try to bring all the important elements together for one technique. We also need to be mindful of our skill; to deliver a "killing" blow over a silly argument on the street is not good for anyone's health. We need control both mentally and physically. This is the spirit of Karate-do.

This philosophy allows us to set very high standards and goals for our training. Other Martial Arts rely on a combination of techniques to win over their attacker but in Karate we aim to finish the fight with one solid technique; this is why we train so hard with each technique. Sometimes, techniques can look very nice and impressive but they aren't developed with 'ikken-hisatsu' philosophy in mind.

# IN HIS OWN WORDS

Grandmaster Azato used to advise to regard our limbs as swords. We could update that advice and remember that knives are easy to buy and conceal. The aim should be to finish the opponent off as quickly as possible – you should always try to knock your opponent out in a real self-defense fight. That is why I still like the idea of training to finish the opponent off with a single technique if your life is at stake even though that might be difficult to do.

**How a teacher should approach these testing for grading students?**

Well, it is definitely a great way to evaluate the progress of the student. As teachers we cannot assume that all students have the same capabilities – physical and mental – and that all of them will have a great technique, balance, power, etc. Each student is unique and based on their personal "uniqueness" we must judge and determine their grade of evolution. We cannot expect that all students can fit into a 40 size suit! Everybody has their own "size" and the teacher has to have this into consideration when evaluating the students in a testing situation.

**You often talk about the importance of the concept of "Ippon-Shobu" in sport competition. Would you elaborate on that please?**

"Ippon-Shobu" exemplifies the very traditional concept of "survival". Its principle teaches us that when we find ourselves in a "life or death" situation there is not time to bounce around like we see in modern competition. It teaches that one mistake can be fatal and that our action must be complete and final to defeat the aggressor or opponent. I understand that under the modern concept of sport competition, the "Ippon-Shobu" may not be the most attractive way of setting a sportive bout but definitely it is the one that keeps the traditional relevance of the duels of the old Samurai. Regardless if a practitioner competes in modern sport events or not, he or she should train and do "Ippon-Shobu" kumite. It brings the sport combat to the very essential aspects of old duel-fighting.

**How was your involvement in the movie "Karate Kid" and your relationship with Pat Johnson?**

Pat Johnson was the stunt coordinator on the film and of course we knew each other from many years in the Martial Arts world. He called me up with the idea of me training actor Pat Morita for his action parts in the film. Pat

# One-on-One with Fumio Demura

allowed me to organize the things and set the choreography the way I wanted. I never had any injuries during the filming and we had a great experience during the shooting time. The only problem was my pants kept splitting every time I had to jump from that fence in one of the fighting scenes!

I was told that they based Mr. Miyagi character on me. It was a great compliment. And I was extremely grateful that I could cooperate and help to make this movie a classic.

**Sensei, you had several health issues. What can you tell us about it?**

I experienced a heart attack when I was working on the television series "Ohara" with Pat Morita. I thought at the time I was just experiencing a really bad cold, but we found out later on that I'd actually had a heart attack while I was on the set. The producer sent me to the hospital right away, so that ended up being it for me on "Ohara". That was actually the first of the heart attacks I've had in my life. I can really say that doing Martial Arts all my life really helped me get through those hard times.

**In our conversations you often talk about the "smaller self" and the "bigger self". Would you please elaborate on that?**

In life things not always go the way we want or expect. It is then when we need to get out of the "smaller self" and see things with a bigger perspective. We need to understand the "bigger picture" and adapt accordingly to the circumstances. In life we are always to face disappointment and frustration but that doesn't mean we won't accomplish our goals. We need to take a step back, get distance and reroute our path to achieve what we have set in the beginning. You have to comprehend both sides of the coin and learn how to move on. And in order to do that we must be aware of the "bigger self" we all have inside of us.

# IN HIS OWN WORDS

**How do you think practitioners can increase their understanding of the spiritual aspect of Karate?**

That is all up to each individual practitioner and their interest. If the person is training in my dojo, I watch him and interview him first to find out what he really wants out of training Karate and then go from there. But new student should be careful with the so-called spiritual aspects of Budo because there is a lot of "fake stuff" in that idea. I don't like to talk too much about it because at the very end it is a personal experience and words can't describe something that you have to discover and feel for yourself. First look into the background of the sensei and see if he is really what he claims to be. If so then, at least you are on the right road.

**How has your personal Karate developed over the years?**

Times change and you have to change with them, after all in nature only those beings who adapt can survive. The training methods are different, the techniques are constantly evolving. You need to find a way to adapt to the ever-changing flow of things. Therefore, you can't get stagnant and stick with the same methods that you used 40 years ago because they won't work. As an instructor, I make sure everything I teach works on the mat and the street. I don't teach things that can get my students hurt because they are useless and ineffective under real circumstances. I want my students to be able to defend themselves and also to compete under sportive rules.

**What is the main human value that you admire?**

Loyalty. These days it seems that people forget they come from and those who helped them along the way. They easily forget and go with the financial security or with whatever is convenient at that moment in time even if that means to betray someone who helped and carried you along the way. In general, I can see that modern society is losing the important values for a decent life. Those values can be found in the old Samurai, their etiquette, their code, their moral principles. I think the world would be much better if we stick to these values. That is why true Martial Arts training and teaching can be very beneficial for our society.

Karate students should remember the little victories that Martial Arts have already helped them achieve. Emphasize the positive and it will help you to move on to your next goal. Never give up! Karate training is not easy, but if you believe strongly enough in yourself, you can achieve anything.

# One-on-One with Fumio Demura

**What are your thoughts on the future of the Martial Arts?**

It is important that we maintain proper standards if the art of Karate is to survive. It would be very sad to see this art become extinct or dilute in a simple sport after just a few generations. Unfortunately, we can't stop people from teaching improper methods and poor standards. We can only ensure that our Karate is of proper technical and moral standards. The teaching of Karate should be geared toward the next generation. Students should focus on the style and quality of instruction they are receiving, and the role models they will have to follow. Karate politics always hurt the students because they suffer for the wants and needs of a few. The reason we got involved and the reason we teach the Martial Arts seems to diminish as people start looking around and concerning themselves with what other people think, "who said what about who", "who is better than anyone else", etc. The idea is to make the art of Karate a way of living life. You set a goal and you accomplish it and work on making it more efficient. If you can accomplish a high level in the Martial Arts, then perhaps nothing is out of reach and your potential is limitless. As a Sensei, your students look to you as a role model and will act similar towards the next generation. Karatekas and martial artists in general, should also understand that instructors, masters, and sensei are just people like themselves. The fact that they may have more knowledge does not make them better than anyone else.

**What do you want the people remember you for?**

I am a karateka. I am a budoka. I want people to remember me as being someone who lived his life based on the principles of Budo and Martial Arts; someone who wanted to share and teach the arts for other human beings to benefit. And I deeply hope my student carry on the essence and principles of the arts of Budo.

**What's your message for all martial artists?**

Never give up. Martial Arts training is not easy, but if you believe strongly enough in yourself, you can achieve anything. For me, that's the greatest part of being an instructor. I don't care about the money. If I help my students to become better human beings, that is the greatest reward.

Don't talk bad about anyone. Train hard and focus on your own training and life. Criticism only brings bad things, and if you spend time looking and worrying about what other people do, you won't be using that time to improve yourself. It's also extremely important give credit to the teachers you learn from. If a man shows you something, give him credit—even if it is only one single technique. Always give credit where credit is due.

One of the most important things these days for the practitioners to understand is Martial Arts is Budo. There is a philosophy in the art that we should all try to keep and develop for the future generations. Respect is paramount in Budo and respect is one of the basis of our society; no respect, no human relationships. Peace can only be achieved through mutual respect among human beings. Unfortunately, the majority of Martial Arts practitioners today are more interested in develop their ability as fighters instead as skill as good human beings. And that's not the right way. All the traditional masters such as Funakoshi Gichin and Jigoro Kano tried to keep the traditional values in the arts they taught. Regardless of the type of physical technique we use, we must strive to keep these values in our lives and Budo training.

**Any final advice?**

Ultimately, the greatest benefit of all Martial Arts training, not only Karate, is self-understanding. Many of the people training Karate never try to understand their own condition or limitations. It is through Karate training that

# One-on-One with Fumio Demura

they can get a clearer picture not only of their own physical abilities, but also of their mental limitations. They will find out by themselves what these are, what they are capable of accomplishing if they put their mind to it, and will want to continue their training. Karate-do training is very similar to life itself. To receive the most out of your training you have to be capable of seeing these similarities.

Train hard but train hard under pressure. They are two different things. Pressure is the key factor that changes everything. Unfortunately, age inevitably diminishes our physical capabilities. Therefore when you are young use your body to train your mind and when you get older...use your mind to train your body.

# SENSEI FUMIO DEMURA
# KARATE TECHNIQUES

Self-defense is a crucial skill and mastering the art of karate can provide you with the knowledge and techniques you need to protect yourself in various situations. In this chapter, we will introduce you to some essential techniques that have been taught and practiced by Fumio Demura Sensei. These techniques serve as a prime example of the principles and strategies he used for practical self-protection. Whether you are a beginner or an experienced martial artist, this comprehensive introduction will provide you with valuable insights and practical skills to enhance your self-defense capabilities.

# IN HIS OWN WORDS

**SHOULDER GRAB:** 1. Aggressor grabs Sensei Demura's right shoulder. 2. Sensei brings his right arm in a clockwise action...3 & 4. And begins to wrap the opponent's arm...5. Until has the arm in a full control. 6. Then, Demura Sensei finishes the aggressor with a palm strike (shotei-uchi) to the face.

# KARATE TECHNIQUES

**DOUBLE LAPEL GRAB:** 1. Aggressor grabs Sensei Demura's both lapels. 2. Sensei brings his right arm upwards and...3....drops it into the opponent's chest as simultaneously brings his left leg back to unbalance the aggressor. 4. From there, Sensei uses a inward block action (soto-uke) to break the grip...5...and smashes his elbow into the aggressor's chest (yoko-uke).

## IN HIS OWN WORDS

**NECK GRAB (Two Hands):** 1. Aggressor grabs Sensei Demura's neck with both hands. 2 & 3. Sensei Demura brings his right arm in a counterclockwise action...4...to break the grip. 5. Then, he attacks with a side elbow strike (yoko-uchi)...6...and continues the counterattack...7...with a knife hand strike to the neck (shuto-uchi).

# KARATE TECHNIQUES

**CROSSED WRIST GRAB (1):** 1. Aggressor grabs Sensei Demura's left wrist. 2. Sensei Demura moves his left leg out of the range and pulls his left arm away from the opponent, unbalancing the aggressor. 3. Then, he moves downward and passes his left arm under the opponent's legs...4...and grabs it with his right hand from the other side. 5. Sensei Demura secures the grip...6...brings his left arm upwards...7...and finishes the opponent off with a downward elbow strike (otoshi-uchi)

## IN HIS OWN WORDS

**CROSSED WRIST GRAB (2):** 1. Aggressor grabs Sensei Demura's right wrist. 2. Sensei moves his right arm in a clockwise action...3... and passes the opponent's arm toward the opposite side unbalancing his stance. 4. Then, he applies pressure and brings the aggressor to the ground...5...where he controls him and...6...finishes off with a punch to the head.

# KARATE TECHNIQUES

**BEAR HUG:** 1. Aggressor grabs Sensei with a bear hug from behind. 2. Sensei Demura drops his body into a 'shiko-dachi' stance and brings his right elbow up to break the grip. 3. Then, he get momentum...4...and applies a back elbow (ushiro-enpi) to the opponent's chest. 5. He grans the opponent's left hand and begins to...6... apply a straight arm lock...7...that brings the aggressor to the ground where he controls him.

## IN HIS OWN WORDS

**FRONT TACKLE:** 1. Aggressor is facing Sensei Demura. 2. The opponent tries to tackle Sensei...3...to what Demura Sensei reacts sprawling with his right leg to create distance as simultaneously places both hands on the shoulder of the aggressor to stop the action.

# KARATE TECHNIQUES

4. Now Sensei grabs the opponent and pulling hard...5...into the ground...6...where he controls him. 7. Then Sensei grabs the aggressor's head and...8...finishes him off.

# FACE OFF WITH
## *FUMIO DEMURA*

**What do you consider your greatest achievement?**

Giving the first professional Karate demonstration in the world.

**What is your idea of perfect happiness?**

Teaching Karate.

**What talent would you most like to have?**

Good acting skills.

**What do you dislike the most?**

Bad attitudes.

**What historical figure do you most identify with?**

"Meiji" from the Samurai era.

**What is your favorite occupation?**

Karate-do.

**What trait do you most deplore in others?**

Bad attitudes.

**What is your favorite journey?**

Anywhere that other people welcome me.

**What do you consider the most overrated virtue?**

There is no such thing as an overrated virtue.

**What is your greatest regret?**

I have none.

**What or who is the greatest love of your life?**

My mother.

**What quality do you like most in a man?**

Strong leadership.

**What is your favorite book?**

One about the history of Japan.

**What thing would you never do?**

Drink or smoke.

**How would you like to die?**

Quick.

# FUMIO DEMURA

# September 15, 1940 – April 24, 2023

# ADDENDUM

In the captivating work of chronicling the life and incredible journey of karate master Fumio Demura, there exists an essential component that adds depth and insight to his remarkable story - an Addendum. This Addendum serves as a treasure trove of wisdom, offering exclusive interviews with his esteemed mentors and teachers, including Ryusho Sakagami, Shigeru Sawabe, and Dan Ivan.

The inclusion of this Addendum holds immense importance as it allows readers to delve into the intricate fabric of Demura Sensei's life in the martial arts. Through these interviews, we are granted a unique opportunity to gain a more profound understanding of who Fumio Demura truly was as a martial artist and as a person.

Ryusho Sakagami, an influential teacher in Demura Sensei's life, shares intimate anecdotes and invaluable lessons learned during their time together. Sakagami's firsthand accounts offer compelling insights into Demura Sensei's growth, challenges faced, and the unwavering dedication that propelled him forward on his martial arts journey.

Shigeru Sawabe, another revered teacher and friend of Demura Sensei, offers his perspective on Fumio's unwavering commitment to honing his craft. Sawabe's teachings shed light on the rigorous training methods employed by Demura Sensei and how they shaped him into the exceptional karate master he became.

Dan Ivan's interview presents us with a unique viewpoint since it was Ivan Sensei who brought Master Demura to the U.S.. His perspective allows us to grasp how Demura Sensei's influence transcends boundaries and impacts individuals beyond his immediate sphere.

In weaving these interviews together, readers are invited on an enlightening expedition. We witness not only Demura Sensei's personal growth but also the vast network of support that has enabled him to achieve greatness. The interviews provide glimpses into moments of vulnerability, triumphs over adversity, and lessons learned along the way.

By including this Addendum in the book, we aim not only to honor the legacy of Fumio Demura but also to inspire aspiring martial artists around the globe. It serves as a testament to the transformative power of mentorship and highlights how influential figures can shape our paths towards greatness.

Ultimately, this additional chapter of the book, allows readers to understand that true mastery is not achieved in isolation but through the guidance and wisdom imparted by mentors and teachers.

# KENWA MABUNI

## The Founder of Shito Ryu

*"When the spirit of karate-do is deeply embraced, it becomes the vehicle in which one is ferried across the great void in order to discover the purpose or meaning of life."* Kenwa Mabuni

# KENWA MABUNI

Kenwa Mabuni was born on November 14, 1889 in the town of Shuri, of the island of Okinawa. A descendant of Onigusikuni, a famous samurai, Mabuni started his studies under the great shuri-te master Yasutsune Itosu (1830-1915) at age 13. Although very weak physically, Mabuni took his training under the 70-year-old master very seriously and progressed quickly, learning over twenty different kata. This training strengthened his body and allowed him to deal with the hard physical demands imposed by his Itosu's rigorous methods. Mabuni practiced under Itosu's guidance for over ten years until Itosu's death. Itosu took a strong linking to his young student and taught him 23 kata.. Legend has it that when Itosu passed away, Mabuni was so sad that he spent a whole year by Itosu's grave, practicing all the kata that Itosu had taught him as a sign of love and devotion toward his teacher.

Before training under naha-te master Kanryo Higashionna (1851-1915), Mabuni went to study under master Gokenki (Wu Xian Gui) who was a tea merchant from Fukien province and teacher of Chinese kempo. Gokenki arrived in Okinawa around 1915, married an Okinawan girl, and taught Fukien-style white crane fist (hakutsuruken) to Mabuni. This Shaolin method featured standing on one leg and yelling "kiai" which was intended to resemble the cry of a crane. This method includes a form named hakkucho that is still practiced in the shito-ryu style all over the world. Later in his life, Gokenki changed his name to Yoshikawa.

Later on, and after the recommendation of his good friend Chojun Miyagi, Mabuni went to study under Higashionna who taught him the method of naha-te. He was pleased with this style of karate because it gave him a different perspective on how to approach training and fighting. Under Higashionna, he perfected the sanchin kata but it was from his studies under Seisho (Kamadeunchu) Arakaki (1840-1918) - who also taught Tsuyoshi Chitose, the founder of Chito Ryu, Gichin Funakoshi of Shoto Kan, and Kanken Toyama of the Shudokan school - that Mabuni Kenwa perfected the kata known today as niseshi, unshu, sochin, aragaki-sai and aragaki-bo.

# The Founder of Shito Ryu

Years later and with the opposition of masters like Kanken Toyama, who considered useless to name the styles with "funny-sounding names", the Dai Nippon Butoku-Kai demanded a more specific description of several group's karate system. Mabuni decided to call his own method hanko ryu (half-hard style) but later he changed the name to shito ryu as a sign of gratitude and respect for his former teachers. The word shito is a combination of shi from Itosu's name and ito from Higashionna's name. Mabuni started teaching students in a local high school as well as to the police in Okinawa where he was working as an officer.

Mabuni combined the two major streams of Okinawa karate and incorporated them into his new style. This gave him a vast store of kata from which to draw. However, he did not just throw a grab-bag style of techniques into a melting pot. He taught pure shuri-te, with it's basic, linear approach to his lower level students, and naha-te to his advanced students. This is the reason why he was highly respected in karate circles as an expert in kata. Master Gichin Funakoshi, a contemporary of Mabuni, not only learned various kata from him but also sent his top student, Masatoshi Nakayama, and his own son, Yoshitaka (Giko) Funakoshi, to Mabuni in order to learn useshi, niseshi, and unshu kata from him. These were later incorporated and modified to fit into his shotokan method as gojushiho, nijushiho, and unsu. Funakoshi described Mabuni as "a leading expert who has collected a myriad of research material and is unsurpassed among others because of his mastery of kata." This

# KENWA MABUNI

is a good proof of the lack of ego shown by the true karate masters. An expert in kata, Mabuni influenced the development of modern shotokan and wado-ryu styles in Japan. Both Funakoshi and Othsuka Hinori looked to him as a source of great knowledge. Unfortunately, many other karate-do teachers envied Mabuni because of how much he knew and his deep level of understanding of the art.

Under master Seisho Arakaki (1840-1918) of Naha, Mabuni also learnt ryukyu kobujutsu, which is the reason why the shito-ryu styles stress the study and training of weapons. He was very interested in a variety of martial arts as well as sports. From these he applied certain athletic training principles to his karate teachings. As a pioneer and innovator, Mabuni developed protector equipment to spar more realistically. He took ideas from kendo, boxing, and baseball and designed protective equipment for kumite training.

Later on he formed the Kenyokukai, a group that would gather at Mabuni's home to research karate history and further technical development. This group was formed by members such as Tokuda Anbun, Gichin Funakoshi, Chibana Chosin, Shiroma Shinpan, Ishikawa Hoko, Oshiro Choju, and Tokumura Seicho. In 1918, Mabuni was granted the honor of demonstrating in the presence of Prince Kuni and Prince Kacho at the Okinawa Normal School. When Funakoshi was sent to Japan to officially introduce Okinawan tode, Mabuni and the research group continued training together.

During his days in Okinawa, Mabuni traveled extensively with his good friend Yasuhiro Konishi, a friend and student who later developed his own

karate system called shindo jinen ryu. In 1925, both Mabuni and Konishi visited Wakayama Prefecture where Kanbun Uechi (founder of Uechi-ryu.) was teaching. After spend a great deal of time with him Mabuni created a kata named shinpa.

Kenwa Mabuni, like other Okinawa teachers, eventually decided to go to Japan to propagate the art of karate. This happened after Jigoro Kano observed a demonstration given by Mabuni Kenwa. The founder of judo told to Mabuni he should go to Japan to spread the art. When Mabuni arrived to Japan, Funakoshi had been in Tokyo for over six years.

# The Founder of Shito Ryu

Out of respect to Funakoshi's seniority in age, Mabuni decided to relocate to Osaka where one of his close friends, Master Motobu, was living already. This was very helpful to Funakoshi Gichin, whose life was already difficult at that time in Tokyo. The establishment of another karate instructor in the area would had made it much harder.

At Donisha University in Osaka, Mabuni taught strictly naha-te on behalf of his close friend Sensei Miyagi, who had taught there before returning to Okinawa. Mabuni strictly adhered to the naha-te method and system. It is interesting to observe that in an advertisement for his book Seipai No Kenkyu Goshijitsu (Hiden Karate-Do Kenpo), originally published in 1934), Mabuni described himself as a shihan of goju ryu. Also, the Otaru newspaper described him as "a great goju-ryu karate-do master." Mabuni also had the intention of finishing a book entitled Goju-Ryu Karate-Do Kempo (Sochin and Kururunfa). From this, it seems more than evident that Mabuni always kept a close link with the art taught by Kanryo Higashionna.

At the beginning of his days in Osaka, he taught at various dojo, including the Seishinkai, school of Kosei Kuniba, who later formed Motobu-ha faction of the shito-ryu style.

For the next few years, Mabuni dedicated himself to the promotion of his karate style in the Osaka area at his Yoshukan dojo. In order to attract people to his school he gave demonstrations where he would break bricks and boards to show the power and effectiveness of karate. With the establishment of the Dai Nihon Karate-do Kai, his enormous efforts began to pay off. As Mabuni's style began to be universally accepted, he started to teach more frequently at both his home and different universities that requested his services.

During the war, many karate masters went through a phase of privations trying to make a decent living. Much more concerned about supporting their families and paying the rent, these masters were much less preoccupied about creating an organization for karate expansion. Mabuni barely survived the post-war turmoil and afterwards devoted himself to the further expansion of shito ryu. It was only after few years after the war, when some universities and colleges began to reopen, that the future of the art was assured. Mabuni always

# KENWA MABUNI

stressed that karate involves three important aspects: shin (heart-spirit), gi (technique) and tai (body). Thus, a good karate-ka should strive to balance the heart, the body, and the physical technique.

Kenwa Mabuni passed away May 23, 1952 at 63 years of age, the same year the American occupation of Japan ended. He never had a chance to witness the economic revival that eventually fueled karate's explosive growth in later years. When he died, Mabuni left behind an impressive group of followers to carry on his legacy: Sakagami Ryusho, Tani Chojiro, Konishi Yasuhiro, Kanei Uechi (not to be confused with Kanei Uechi of Uechi-ryu) Iwata Manzo, Yoshiaki Tsujikawa, Kuniba Kosei, Hisatomi Tokio and also his sons Kenzo Mabuni and Kenei Mabuni. Kenei, Kenwa's oldest son, joined forces with Tokyo University graduates Manzo Iwata and Ken Saiko and created the World Shito Kai Karate-do Federation with headquarters in the Honbu dojo in Tokyo. Kenzo Mabuni, the youngest son, was asked by his mother Kamae Mabuni and numerous karate seniors to take over the style. Unsure about his final decision, Kenzo Mabuni went into seclusion in the city of Nagoya. He trained diligently for over two years retreat and spent some time training with Ryusho Sakagami and Watanabe Kenichi. After this he decided to accept and fully commit himself to the task of being the inheritor of his father's lineage.

# The Founder of Shito Ryu

Kenzo Mabuni lived in the original family home in Osaka, where he had the headquarters of the "Nippon Karate Do Kai". He kept the founder's syllabus, personnal technical notes, textbooks and records. He felt that his mission was to teach what his father left for the world. He passed away on June 26th, 2005 and was recognized as the true heir of his father's art.

Although Kenwa Mabuni authored several books and manuscripts, all of his books were already out of print before the war and were never translated into English. In like manner, some of his manuscripts are untraceable. After the acknowledgement of his tremendous influence and contribution to the modern world of karate-do, some of his works have been reprinted in Japanese.

After the death of Kenwa Mabuni, the shito-ryu style became one of the four most practiced karate systems in the world and is considered as the true repository of traditional kata. Although Kenzo Mabuni was the only one who kept the style pure as his father taught it, different branches of the art such as tani-ha shito-ryu (shukokai), hayashi-ha shito-ryu, seishin kai, motobu-ha shito-ryu, itosu-kai, and shito-kai spread his original message in slightly different forms – but all of them retain the essence of a great karate master named Kenwa Mabuni.

# RYUSHO SAKAGAMI

## THE GENTLE MASTER

Ryusho Sakagami exemplified all the qualities a master of Budo should. Born on 1915 in Kawanishi City, which is in the Hyugo Prefecture, Sakagami Sensei began his martial art training at age 10. The Nihon Budo Kyogi-Kai gave him the highest Budo award — the Budo Koro-Sho medal. His extensive training in the art of karate-do under grandmasters of the caliber of Choki Motobu and Kenwa Mabuni, among others, made him one of the top and more knowledgeable masters of his generation. With an extensive training in judo, iaido, kendo and kobudo, Sakagami Sensei used the Budo principles and his education to lead an honorable life. He stayed active at his dojo in Tsurumi Ward, between Yokohama and Kawasaki, until his very last days of life. His teacher, Shito-Ryu founder Kenwa Mabuni, asked Ryusho Sakagami to succeed him in the heritage of Itosu Anko's orthodox method of karate, appointing him the third generation leader of the Itosu-ha seito.

In 1980, the Federation of All-Japan Karate-Do Organizations awarded Master Sakagami his 8th dan in karate-do, and in 1987 he received his 8th dan in Muso Jikiden Eishin Ryu iaido.

The most important karate federations in the world acknowledged Grandmaster Sakagami to be a living treasure and a repository of the history and knowledge of Budo. Ryusho Sakagami — a true legend of the art of karate, an honorable human being and a gentle master — died from heart failure on December 28, 1993.

81

# RYUSHO SAKAGAMI

**Q: Master Sakagami, please tell us about your beginnings in the art.**

A: My grandfather was a kendo master. I trained in iaido under Nakayama Hiromichi Sensei, who was a meijin, and in aikido under Hirai Minoru Sensei, who was a direct student of O'Sensei Ueshiba. I traveled often to Okinawa – though my parents didn't know it – to train in karate, because I was informed that there was an excellent master in Osaka. His name was Kenwa Mabuni, and I began my training under him around 1935. Training at that time was very different than today. I also trained under Choki Motobu. I have also trained in judo, jodo, koBudo and other classical arts of Budo.

**Q: Did you meet Funakoshi Gichin Sensei?**

A: Yes I did. He visited Mabuni Sensei, and he had some of his students learn kata from Mabuni Sensei. Later on, they modified things to better fit the style Funakoshi Sensei was developing. Mabuni Sensei had a good relationship with Funakoshi Sensei.

**Q: Why did you take over the Itosu-kai heritage after becoming one of the oldest students of Kenwa Mabuni Sensei?**

A: Mabuni Sensei was the founder of Shito-ryu, which is a combination of naha-te, shuri-te and tomari-te. In Japan, the son is always the heir to his father's throne. Mabuni Kenei, although a junior to me, had to be the leader of his father's heritage. Kenwa Mabuni Sensei, knowing that I was a senior, suggested that I carry on with the tradition of the Itosu-ha, which I honored and accepted. Mabuni Sensei learned from Master Itosu Ankho. Master Itosu was the teacher of other great masters like Chosin Chibana, Funakoshi Gichin, Choki Motobu, et cetera. For me, it was a privilege and an honor.

# The Gentle Master

**Q: Master Sakagami, how much influence of Zen is there in Bushido as a code of the samurai and Budo?**

A: The spirit underlying the arts practiced by the samurai was part Shinto and part Zen. This discipline was adapted from the Zen monastery and imposed on the martial arts elements and training. The most mundane act was to be performed with the utmost perfection. That ritual and tedious repetition in training provided not only technical expertise for the warriors but also a spiritual connection to the ancestors.

**Q: How do you feel after so many years of training?**

A: I feel great about myself, but I'd probably be better if I had had more knowledge of the human body and proper nutrition. Knowing what I know today, I would have suffered fewer injuries and could have trained harder. To make their training and life more productive, new generations should study all of the information they have today. With that, they should be able to go farther than we old teachers did. In doing a martial art, the mind, spirit and technique should all be fully expressed. If your technique is correct and your mind and spirit fully expressed and arrived, you will progress very fast. In this case, you will get a different feeling everyday. Students should carefully realize this. If your technique, your mind and your spirit do not arrive, you are wasting your time and will never succeed.

# RYUSHO SAKAGAMI

**Q: What should be the main principles on which training is based?**

A: All forms of martial arts start with courtesy and respect. The main idea of Budo is to remove all arrogance and pomposity and replace them with humbleness and the right spirit, and it's important to display those qualities that were established and sustained by generations of dedicated and devoted martial artists. The true Budo spirit is not something that you can put on and take off at will. It is something you become. It is in everything you do and permeates through all your acts. It puts us in accord with the flow of the universe. It is true that the value of a martial art depends on its application, but the goal is not always self-defense or self-protection. There are some other higher goals in Budo training. In a true martial artist, all of the actions are geared [or designed] so that there is no dishonor or loss of face. The most important thing to keep in mind is that all forms of Budo are not courses of study, but rather, a way of life.

**Q: Sensei, what do you think is the most important thing a teacher should make sure the students learn, and what is the most relevant principle the student should keep in mind?**

A: It is important that a martial art instructor foster a sense of self-responsibility in his students. For the students, the best way to learn is to practice, persevere and think about the intent behind the technique. It is too easy to look for magic while the real secret is sweat. There is no magic in the martial arts, just a good teacher and a lot of hard work. The key is to practice, and I have always been an advocate for teaching the students everything I know. Holding back just weakens the art. The old principle of saving a little, which implies not teaching the whole art, has caused the deterioration of the martial arts.

**Q: Do you think a certain amount of knowledge is lost when the art is taught from generation to generation?**

A: Yes. The reason that techniques are lost is not because the teacher withholds the knowledge. Instead, it's because today's students don't work to understand what lies behind the physical movements. Sometimes you have a situation in which there are two students, and you spend a lot of time and effort on them. One turns out to be very good and the other turns out poor. The martial arts are not something you can copy. You must learn what lies behind the technique. The martial arts are taught today only like a good

# The Gentle Master

physical exercise. Unfortunately, they are lacking the true Budo spirit. The training is not geared to a real life-or-death situation, and this single fact changes the whole approach.

A student should be humble and honest with himself, because he should know his limitations and true possibilities. The martial arts are great as a physical exercise, as well as an excellent vehicle for mental health. Anyone should be able to become strong and more confident if he trains with the proper direction and goals in mind. Don't expect miracles though, because the martial arts won't bring any kind of mystical powers! It is important that a martial art instructor foster a sense of self-responsibility on the part of his students.

**Q: Is it correct to change elements of the art and modify things that our teachers taught us?**

A: I don't advocate change for change's sake, and this is what has happened recently in the world of martial arts. People with a limited amount of knowledge put together a little of this, a little of that, give it a new name and [suddenly] we have a new, complete martial art system that will liberate all the practitioners in the world from the useless, traditional methods. I feel sorry for those students [who train with them] for not knowing any better. They follow these "instructors" and give them their money and their time. The traditional styles were put together with a sense of balance. Everything in a particular style was designed and glued together with meaning and reason. The techniques, the strategies and the principles found in the forms, et cetera, [all] work perfectly together like the pieces of a puzzle. If you have all the pieces and keep the final puzzle as it meant to be, you'll have a nice picture

# RYUSHO SAKAGAMI

once you are finished. On the contrary, if you try to mix pieces from several different puzzles, you'll have a mess with no foundation and no reason to exist. People who do this often show big contradictions; they spend too much time repeating the words of other martial artist because they have nothing to offer and no central philosophy in what they are trying to teach. The old masters weren't so naive when they designed the different styles. Give them the credit they deserve because there is more in the traditional styles than what meets the eye. These martial artists who create new styles operate under the misconception that they are creating a perfect fighting method. To me, this concept is simply an illusion. The perfect style doesn't exit. Perfection is something that sounds very good, but it is unattainable. By simply eliminating classical techniques and replacing them with boxing does not make a new method better or superior. It makes it different. That's all. By changing the old styles and thinking that we have developed a superior method, we are creating a foundation for failure because that's another illusion. There is no perfect person, and there is no perfect style but the one that fits you and brings understanding and a peaceful spirit to your existence as a human being.

**Q: Many people criticize the martial arts because they are loaded with rituals and protocols that are not necessary in the West. What is your opinion?**

A: The martial arts are more than fighting. In Japan, they are part of Budo. In China, they represent a way of life and a way of thinking that involves the principles of Taoism, and the same happens in every place where the arts were developed. Protocol and rituals have very little to do with the actual fighting, but they are vehicles to preserve education, politeness, etiquette, et cetera. All these are very important values for a student. The people who criticize this simply don't have the knowledge of what these aspects represent. The cour-

# The Gentle Master

tesy and proper protocol found in the traditional schools are the essence of the education. They are the true bones of what's happening and keep everything within a serious environment for education. When you take away the protocol, the rituals like bowing and paying respect to your opponent, you are taking away from the history, from the legacy, from the bones and the essence of what a true martial art is all about. People should learn to differentiate between the rituals and the essence represented in these rituals. Maybe then they will realize why they are so important for the future generations.

**Q: How important are the basics?**

A: The technical foundations, which were dwelled upon for years, are unfortunately and often glossed over in a matter of a few months of part-time work. It is very important to train hard in the basics of the art. Never ignore these. Forms are composed of single movements or parts that make up the whole form. To become an expert, you should strive to learn how to use these parts. The basics, which are known as kihon, apply to the art of karate-do, as well as to the foundations of Budo. It is very misleading [and wrong] if you move on and never give the basics another thought once you have learned them. To keep the foundation strong, you always have to go back to it, regardless of how many years of practice you have accumulated.

**Q: Sensei, what kind of additional training is helpful for karate?**

A: Traditionally, we had a series of supplementary training aids. They are classical implements that helped karateka to strengthen their bodies and prepare them for combat. The makiwara is one of them. Kobudo training also helps the wrists and hands.

# RYUSHO SAKAGAMI

**Q: Is makiwara training beneficial for a practitioner?**

A: If the student is guided by a knowledgeable teacher, it is definitely positive. You don't want to hit the makiwara without having a previous understanding and knowledge of what your goals are. You need to know the purpose of [training with the] makiwara, and the purpose is not to develop calloused hands. That's simply a consequence of the training. Your body, through correct training in the makiwara, will learn how to absorb the energy sent back to it after your fist hits an object. Thus, you will learn how to develop the right positioning when hitting an object with full force. It is a different [phenomena] to practice your punches and kicks in the air than it is to hit a solid object. The positioning of your legs, hip, back, shoulder, elbow, forearm and wrist must be properly aligned to exert all the possible power from your body and to absorb the shock of the impact. Basically, makiwara teaches you the right technique. If you do makiwara training simply to develop big knuckles and calluses, you won't get any benefit from it because that's not the purpose.

**Q: Does the sportive approach change the teacher/student relationship?**

A: Well, unfortunately, many people today think that karate is a sport, so they train for specific tournaments and competition, pretty much the same

# The Gentle Master

way that a basketball or football player trains for a game. Because the goal for every training session relates to sport competition, the person training them, correcting their movements and guiding them is a trainer or coach. Never a sensei. The word sensei has very different connotations and meanings that extend way beyond winning a tournament. There are no coaches or trainers in Budo.

The person who teaches you to discover yourself and your place in the world is not a coach. He is called teacher, master or sensei. He teaches you loyalty, courtesy, etiquette and all the important values that make a person a better human being. The person who trains a boxer is a trainer; the individual who trains and teach a karate-ka is a sensei. If the training is focused to win tournaments in a sport environment, other important qualities intrinsic in the true Budo training, such as courtesy, loyalty, et cetera, are simply lost and forgotten. There can be an appreciation and respect for your coach but not in a Budo way. Etiquette and proper attitude disappear. That's why we see coaches and competitors complaining constantly in a tournament if a referee's decision doesn't go their way. Proper etiquette is lost. Style is not as important as the spirit of the art.

**Q: Is there anything you would like to add?**

A: Yes, dedicate yourself to reach the higher levels of Budo and put your heart and soul into it. The key to understanding the art of karate-do and most other Budo arts is the underlying philosophy that runs so inseparably through all the forms of Japanese life. The principles of karate are based on the principles of life and the universe. It is the realization of an existing phenomenon – such as a punch or a kick – that gives meaning to that phenomenon, and it is the understanding of that meaning that allows one to master the phenomenon. It is for this purpose – understanding – that a person learns the art of karate-do.

# DAN IVAN

## Karate's Enduring Spirit

A half-century of budo experience was contained within this Old-World gentleman who was responsible for bringing some of the greatest Japanese karate masters of all time to the United States. A criminal investigator with the U.S. military occupational force in Japan after WWII, Ivan was one of the first Westerners to forget the hatred of the war. And to start building bridges by studying karate with his former enemies. Ignoring the harsh words of Eastern and Western critics who questioned his openness, Ivan's strength of character and strong personal morals enabled him to forge friendships with many of the top martial arts masters of shattered post-war Japan that last until this day.

Sensei Ivan was looked upon as an example of understanding, patience, and tolerance. Humble, charming, and knowledgeable, Ivan was an American icon. His training under such notables as Isao Obata, Gogen Yamaguchi, Gozo Shioda, and Ryusho Sakagami — just to name a few — makes practitioners around the world, who would give up their firstborn for 10 percent of this man's experiences, look at him with healthy envy.

Ivan enjoyed sharing his experiences and knowledge with those lucky enough to come in contact with him. He was one of the most treasured martial artists of the Western world.

# DAN IVAN

**Q: How long have you been practicing the martial arts?**

A: Formally since 1948, when I was stationed in Japan. Prior to that, in 1945, I had WWII military unarmed-combat training which peaked my interest. In those early years I earned black belts in karate, judo, aikido and kendo. I've heard people in Japan say that I was the first foreigner to do this in the four major budo arts. In karate, my training was mostly in shotokan, shito-ryu, a little goju-ryu and wado-ryu, plus a taste of some lesser known arts.

**Q: How many styles have you trained in and who were your first teachers?**

A: My very first teachers were from the Kudokan – most notable were Mifune and Ito, both 10th dan, Meijin, then my close friend, Sato, a close friend, and Ishikawa, a two-year judo champion in Japan and many others. In karate my first instructor was Isao Obata, first disciple under Master Funakoshi; also I started goju-ryu with Gogen Yamaguchi, but stopped when the Kodokan asked me to. In those early years after the war, Yamaguchi and others were struggling and not yet well accepted – while Obata was. At the JKA, it was Chief Nakayama and Sensei Kase. Most significant to my shotokan training was Kenji Yamamoto from Hosei University and one of JKA's main sensei; this was after about two years with Obata who really give me my foundation. Over the years, many other JKA sensei added a lot to my knowledge. One of my greatest sensei and an inspiration to me was shito-ryu master Ryusho Sakagami. This man was a dictionary of kata and a great, but humble person. Also, a tough old sensei, Yamada, who taught the yakuza and also professional bodyguards. He brought a whole different dimension to Karate than did the others. I can't forget another prominent goju-ryu master – Izumigawa. I know I am probably forgetting someone, but I learned from so many because of my military situation. I was stationed in different parts of Japan due to my assignment as a criminal investigator.

# Karate's Enduring Spirit

In aikido, my sensei was Gozo Shioda, head of Yoshinkai; a man small in stature but with fantastic technique. He and his staff helped me and other agents in our office to cope with handling criminal suspects in a more humane way. My kendo training was with the Japan Kendo Federation and their instructors. Kendo was at the time the most organized group. Sensei Saeki, who was a descendent of a true Samurai family, was my main teacher and mentor. There were many other arts and sensei that I had the privilege of training with. In the beginning the physical movements were not all that difficult for me. Kicking with precision was different than street-fighting kicks, and learning to punch with a bare hand was different than boxing with gloves – but overall, it was enjoyable.

**Q: How did Westerners respond to your traditional Japanese training?**

A: In the early days, there was a lot of hostility in Japan against Americans; however, in the dojo it was not too apparent. As a matter of fact martial arts helped to bridge this hostility. I recall being called a "Jap lover" because I hung out with my new friends and sensei. I am sure that they were also getting the same treatment for hanging out with me. Eventually, all this passed. Westerners loved Japanese martial arts. There were not a whole lot of us, but those that did train did it because they really took to it. There were eventually more men taking karate than judo, and fewer took kendo; but as time went on, Westerners begin taking iaido, even more than kendo.

**Q: How has your personal karate changed and developed over the years?**

A: Like anyone else, my first years were cramming in all the training I could, jumping in with both feet, not really stopping to analyze techniques. Then, as the years went on, I begin to realize the dynamics and principles of proper kicking and striking. You learn that when something is executed the right way, you can cause more damage with your technique.

Even today, after producing over 135 videos of masters in all arts, Chinese, Korean, Japanese, Okinawan, Philippine and others, I realized no man can ever learn it all because there are so many fascinating angles to all these arts. I wish I had another one or two lifetimes ahead of me. There are many new things to do and try in so many different arts. You should concentrate on one and make it your foundation, but other arts have much to offer.

# DAN IVAN

**Q: What were the most important points of your teaching days?**

A: At first, I began teaching to have someone to train with. There were hardly any martial artists around. Then I had a wake-up call. I realized that men, women, and children were coming to me and I was responsible for them. If you are sincere and you are teaching properly, they will come to you, and, like it or not, you are guiding and influencing their lives – a major responsibility that I took seriously. I actually changed from having personal selfish goals of doing karate – now I had to do it for my students.

**Q: With all the technical changes during the last 30 years, do you think there is still "pure" shotokan, shito ryu, et cetera?**

A: Different styles or ryu, add competition and interest. Each style feeds off the other and learns from the other, so it's good. From fifty years ago, I see many styles that you could only distinguish from the kata, but the basics are very similar. We don't want to become too generic, so lets keep our separate styles that include our history and traditions. Purists in the martial arts, especially karate, are rare and becoming almost extinct. Influences today change the way we teach, and what we teach; however, there are still a handful of sensei that flow with the times and still manage to maintain the true art with the right spirit and attitude.

**Q: Do you think that Western karate has caught up with Japanese karate?**

A: If you monitor the world karate events, you'll see that the Japanese no longer dominate the sport. This is regulated competition, of course, but if you look at true budo and non-sport karate, I think you will still find Japan still has the edge. Karate has evolved into a sport, like it or not. And as a sport it has attracted far more students. But there are still a rare few schools out there that disregard this part of training and teach the old way, which is technique, self-defense and personal development. The winners in this struggle are those that can do it all – the sport and the traditional training – even though it is a very difficult balance to strike.

**Q: Do you feel that there are any fundamental differences in karateka from different ethnic or cultural backgrounds?**

A: All of us – all races – have the same body. The deciding factor is your size, your physical conditioning, and your length of training. There is one area that the Japanese might have an edge – the college years. In Japan, karate is

# Karate's Enduring Spirit

part of the curriculum at most colleges and universities. A young man can train every day, two to four hours, for his entire four years in school. So, for the 18 to 22-year-olds it is an advantage because you won't find many schools that keep up this regimen.

**Q: Do you think it helps karateka to train with weapons?**

A: Training with weapons is another dimension – another road to take for more dexterity and coordination. It is part of the total art and stimulating to practice.

**Q: What's your opinion of the makiwara and other supplemental training devices?**

A: Makiwara training has been replaced by the heavy bag. Remember, the makiwara was invented because in early times, and in poor times in postwar Japan, they didn't have money or equipment. Makiwara or bag training is something you must do, otherwise you never know that your wrist might be weak and your hand might collapse when you punch; or if you don't kick properly you can twist an ankle. Supplemental training -weights, running, swimming, and other sports, is good to help build your body. Don't forget, we live with TV and automobiles and generally live a soft life; so we should exert ourselves at every opportunity. Besides, young people have growing bodies. So the more varied exercise they get, the better it is.

**Q: Do you think a sensei's personal training should be different from those he teaches?**

A: It's hard to teach and train at the same time. If you train alongside your students, how can you correct them? And this is the responsibility of the sensei, to correct his students. Some training can be done with them, but as a sensei, you must make separate time for yourself to portray the technique or kata to the class. Get rid of your bad habits or your class will emulate them. Definitely, both things have to be taken care of separately.

# DAN IVAN

**Q: What is the most important element of karate teaching: self-defense, sport, or tradition?**

A: Lot of basics and sparring techniques are probably first, then kata, and then sport techniques for those in the class that attend sport tournaments. Too many groups are striving to win tournaments and are neglecting good, solid training which improves your overall ability. Kata should take up about a third, or maybe only a fourth of the training; the rest should be kumite, basics, and self-defense.

**Q: Some people think that going to Japan to train is highly necessary; do you share this view?**

A: Going to Japan to train is highly motivational due to the atmosphere and the entire attitude. And you can find good old-fashioned dojo there and solid training; but as far as being highly necessary, perhaps it is not that way anymore since we do have some very capable sensei here, both American and Japanese. Karate changed in a major way after World War II, when myself and other GIs were stationed there. Early training was more combative, since Japan had just come out of about a fifty-year war. The attitude was a more severe war mentality, training was more serious and it took year for us to quit training and teaching as if we were going into life and death combat. Today, there are countless deadly techniques not taught or even known by modern sensei – both in Japan and around the world. Kids and women are now widely accepted; this was not allowed after the war because what we taught was for men that might have to face mortal enemies. Today, sport has emerged strongly and allows all ages and sexes to participate. But I do long for the old days of true budo.

**Q: Who would you like to have trained with?**

A: Actually, I sought out who I wanted, so actually there are perhaps only a couple of men I wish I had developed a relationship with that I didn't. One is Grandmaster Ueshiba and the other is Grandmaster Funakoshi. Both were present at many events being held in those early days, but I never had the privilege of taking any classes with them. When I was new to the arts in the 1940s and '50s, these masters were pointed out to me, but I was too stupid to be impressed – and it was only after many years that I realized these men were founding icons.

**Q: What would you say to someone who is interested in learning karate-do?**

A: If you are interested in the art, visit some schools and observe. See the quality and look closely at the physical skills of the students; but just as important look closely at their attitude and manners. Listen to the facts, not a sales pitch. Karate is growing, and there are good schools out there turning out good students. Overall, the true sensei – the traditionalist – survives and thrives. If they fall by the wayside, they are not ready to be sensei or perhaps just not capable. A good school depends on a good sensei. A lot of lumps and bruises will happen along the way, but stick to it. What's your alternative, watching TV? Do it – bring in the whole family. There's room for everyone in karate and that's what makes it so special.

**Q: Do you think engaging in free-fighting is necessary to achieving good street-fighting skills?**

A: Free-fighting is really important, whether you do it with equipment or without. It gives you speed, timing, and distancing that you can use if someone attacks you. Good free-fighters can simply outmaneuver the average person that comes swinging and kicking wildly.

**Q: What is your opinion about mixing karate styles?**

A: Mixing karate styles won't hurt, but you absolutely must concentrate heavily only on one for more efficient advanced in knowledge. As time goes on you will find many similarities in the arts – the single biggest difference is kata. In fact, today in major tournaments and events you will often see a shotokan stylist doing a goju kata, or shito-ryu student using a shotokan technique. Overall, more knowledge is good for you if you get solid roots in one system first.

**Q: Modern karate is moving away from bunkai, or applications, in kata practice. How important is bunkai for understanding kata and karate-do in general?**

A: Kata bunkai is good and necessary. Translating a kata is something very challenging. Most of the challenge is in asking yourself, "What the hell is this move for?" Simple blocks, strikes, and kicks in kata are easy to see and understand; but frankly there are many moves handed down from centuries ago that are perplexing. Over the years I have watched many so-called "high-ranking masters" perform many different bunkai to the same kata. And this is not wrong. You can devise applications any way you want in many cases, keeping in mind that whoever originated a particular kata was influenced by certain weapons of his era and certain circumstances in fighting. Some of these circumstances are lost to us today, so we do the best we can.

**Q: What is the philosophical basis for your karate training?**

A: That's a hard one. My motivation and even my philosophy was to elevate my physical and mental stature. Martial arts does that while you're training without having to think about it. One day, despite all the hard knocks, you feel mentally and physically stronger – and this is something to be cherished no matter what your age or status in life. Personally, I didn't have much of a spiritual view of karate until after decades of training. My brain works slower than others perhaps, but it took me years to realize that karate was more than fighting movements, and that I was much stronger mentally than physically. You can meditate, read up on lives of the masters, and so forth, but the spiritual aspects have to grow on you. I don't think you can just look for it and find it. It has to exist as a seed within you that can grow later on. Besides karate being an invaluable aid in working the streets of Tokyo, it also was motivational to feel my improvement as the years went on, and also to see my students achieve status in the martial arts world. Things like these inspire me even today.

# Karate's Enduring Spirit

**Q: What keeps you motivated after all these years?**

A: As you grow older and as you teach, your training becomes less intense – or at least you have less time to train – so you do what you can because you can't keep the same pace you had when you were young and unencumbered with teaching or raising a family. Make a little time every day, or every other day, even if you are training alone, work the muscles for kicks and  strikes, and do some kata. Your lifestyle, age, and available time will dictate how much you'll be able to do. A mistake many people make is that because they can't do what they did before, they drop out. This is not wise. The practitioner has to make adjustments and do the best they can. The motivation for training in the first place is different. During my prime training years, the world was coming out of a depression and a war, and hardships made hard men and women. Today this condition doesn't exist; so with few exceptions, students are a lot softer mentally and physically. Nevertheless, they can still be as dedicated and sincere about their training and achieve impressive results if they have the right sensei. The practice of karate offers you a path to achievement in a deep, personal sense – it's something you have that can't be taken away. Even away from practice, this attitude always stays with you. It may be not evident for a long period of time but it will emerge when you need it the most. At my age, watching the skill of good practitioners is so inspiring. Martial artists of all styles are truly fascinating to watch if they are skilled. Remember the recent Olympics? Although you may not be a high diver, watching them was great – and to see our American heavyweight in his wrestling win over the Russian champion was great. So, my motivation is staying in the best condition I can at my age, and watching and associating with good sensei and students.

# DAN IVAN

**Q: You invited Fumio Demura to come to the U.S. Can you tell us a little bit about it?**

A: Of course! During my time in Japan, when I was planning to get back to the U.S. I thought about the possibility of bringing a good karate instructor from Japan to help me to spread the art. At that time I was training under Ryusho Sakagami – who was a direct student of Shito Ryu founder, Kenwa Mabuni. In the beginning I was thinking about inviting some instructor from the J.K.A. but my good friend Don F. Draeger had a long talk with me and explained me some things that made a lot of sense. Therefore, I decided to ask Ryusho Sakagami Sensei about who would be interested to come to the U.S..

Sakagami Sensei asked to some students at the dojo and Fumio Demura said he would do it.

**Q: Did he speak any English at the time?**

A: None! It was funny because his English was non-existent! But I saw a big determination and passion for what it was in front of him. I knew the language was not going to be a problem at all. A young Demura loved the possibiity and he accepted my offer and moved to the U.S.

**Q: How were his first days in America?**

A: It took a while for him to adapt but that was normal. Little by little his English got better and he was able to communicate with the students better. In the beginning, it was hard for him but he had a very strong determination to accomplish his goals. He basically taught by showing with his body how the technique should be performed! I remember teaching him basic words like "forward", "backward" "hip" "turn", "relax", etc

**Q: He was a Shito Ryu practitioner and you we teaching Shotkoan. How did you two manage this at the Santa Ana dojo?**

A: He learnt the Shotokan style out of respect for me. So during a period of time he taught the Shotokan aspects of karate but he included – in some ways

# Karate's Enduring Spirit

- the style he learnt from Ryusho Sakagami Sensei. So we can say that it was a mixture of both styles...We never mixed kata at all but the technical fundation – that we had at the dojo - was very interesting because we combined the essential principles and concepts of Shotokan and Shito Ryu in one package.

**Q: What are the most important attributes of a student?**

A: A student need to be prepared to learn even before the actual learning process begins; this is one of the most important aspects in traditional martial arts training. Of course, the key words are "dedication" and "hard work." It sounds cliche, but that's what it takes: dedication and hard work over and above anything else you might do. One of the most important qualities for a student is the ability to listen and try really hard – to master one simple technique at a time, not try to advance too fast and overlook basics. Training becomes hard as you go along; more is expected of you as you advance in grade. As the pressure mounts you must meet this challenge as you would in any sport. Karate differs from all other activities because you should always be working against yourself, not others; so if you slow down or stop, you will find it harder to continue again.

**Q: There has been very little written about you in magazines. Why do you obviously not thrive on publicity?**

A: Maybe it's my prior military experience of working undercover on criminal cases, and then working military intelligence – being inconspicuous and overlooked was vital to survival. But then again, I never liked loudmouths and braggarts, so it's my nature to be happy in the background. But I've had my share of publicity. When I was younger I was in over a dozen martial arts magazines, including Inside Kung Fu and Black Belt, and I wrote hundreds of articles on the martial arts. But fame and publicity are fleeting – your inner soul and your spirit are what endures.

# SHIGERU SAWABE

## A LEGACY OF EXCELLENCE

A direct student of both Kenwa Mabuni and Ryusho Sakagami, Sawabe Shihan kept the essence of the valuable teachings he received from these legendary masters of Budo pure. "Karate is not a sport. It should be used for self-defense as a last resort only. Karate-do is a way of life ... a means to achieve security and fearlessness." As well as his career as leader of Japan's largest corporate security company, he was a leader in Japanese Karate-Do and held several top positions with several karate-do's governing bodies. He also authored several highly regarded texts on karate and was the leader of the Japan Karate-Do Shubu-kai. Sawabe Shihan remained active and eager to share the gifts he received from his masters and epitomized the true definition of the "warrior spirit." In his teaching, he always stressed that as one gets older continuous training becomes increasingly important. And, although he was considered among the most knowledgeable of living karate masters, Shigeru Sawabe remembered us all that he had not arrived to the final destination in the journey of Budo.

103

# SHIGERU SAWABE

### Q: When did you first meet Sakagami Ryusho?

A: I met Sakagami Sensei during wartime. I was in junior high school at the time. At that time in school we were required to do either judo or kendo. I chose kendo, and Sakagami Sensei was the kendo teacher. One day I saw Sakagami Sensei punching a tree. I asked him what he was doing, and he told me that he was practicing karate. Not long afterward I enlisted two of my friends, and we asked Sakagami Sensei to teach us. After the war in 1945, General

MacArthur banned the practice of martial arts and Sakagami Sensei decided to stop teaching. After several months, my friends and I found where Sakagami Sensei lived. We went there and asked him to keep teaching us karate. We had to insist a little, but he finally agreed.

### Q: How were you introduced to Mabuni Kenwa?

A: Sakagami Sensei took me to Mabuni Sensei's dojo; that's how I met him. I continued studying karate-do with both Sakagami Sensei and Mabuni Sensei. After high school, I entered Osaka Kogyo University, where Mabuni Sensei was the instructor. I trained with the university club during the day and at night went to Mabuni Sensei's dojo to train more. During my third year at the University, Mabuni Sensei passed away. After that, I continued my training with Sakagami Sensei at his dojo. At that time, his dojo was located at his home.

### Q: How was the training under these two great karate masters?

A: The training under Sakagami Sensei and Mabuni Sensei was very different compared to what we see today in any martial arts school. During the war, when I began, we had no gi and no dojo. We just trained outside. We trained barefoot even when it was quite cold with snow on the ground. The main thing then was the constant training. I would train for three hours at the university and then take the train to Mabuni Sensei's dojo for more training. The morale and mentality after the war dictated how all the practitioners felt

# A Legacy of Excellence

and how dedicated they were to the training. It is difficult to explain, but there were mixed feeling inside each and every one of us. From the technical point of view, we weren't concerned about sport and our kata training was a method of training and researching for the most efficient self-defense techniques.

**Q: How was the approach to kata training?**

A: Well, to begin with, we didn't really care at all about the look of our kata. This is something that you see today. At that time, kata was not for show. By this, I mean that we never tried to make it look good. It was like a textbook in which you could take technical information. The essence and meaning behind the form were the most important things. The outside or mold was simply perfected to match the proper delivery of the physical technique.

**Q: Can you give us an example?**

A: Sure. When we did shuto-uke, we did not hold our fingers perfectly straight. The idea behind shuto-uke is to use the outside edge of your hand to block or hit; therefore, if you straighten all of your fingers, you take force away from that specific area of the hand. We kept the fingers bent to focus more of the tension in that zone. The movement doesn't look as pretty as the "perfect" straight hand, but it is the correct way of doing it …when you are doing it for real use.

The technical approach to the movements was more natural and the human body was taken more into consideration. The main idea in fighting was not to score a point based on speed and power. Instead, it was to attack the vital points in the opponent's body. This is the reason why we develop each part of our body as a weapon. We used fingers to the eyes ands throat, side of the hand to the neck, instep to the groin, kicks to the legs and every other technique that allowed us to seriously hurt the opponent. That's how we learned karate. It was a method of self-defense and not a sport.

**Q: Are you against sport in karate?**

A: No, I am not as long as the true spirit of the Budo stays during practice and training. Sport can be seen as a small part of the whole art called karate. That small part never is more important than the art.

**Q: How do you remember Mabuni Kenwa?**

A: He was a very special individual. His goal was to try to gather as much knowledge as possible, and that's the reason why he studied so many styles and accumulated so many kata. I understand that modern practitioners do not need to study 60 or 70 kata, but Mabuni Sensei was in a very important position in the history of Budo. He was the link between several styles in Okinawa and the acceptance of karate in Japan. He was in a very important position, and he had to communicate and impart the knowledge in a proper way with the right information. He became a repository of traditional knowledge and kata and many other outstanding karate masters went to him for study and advice. For instance, Master Funakoshi studied with him and sent several of his main students [including M. Nakayama Sensei] to learn from Mabuni Kenwa. He was highly respected among all karate teachers and masters of his time.

**Q: And Sakagami Ryusho?**

A: He was a very special individual. His knowledge of Budo was outstanding. Not only he was a master in karate but also in other arts like aikido, kendo koBudo and iaido. He trained with some of the best teachers ever and his understanding of how the different arts fit together in the perfect format for a Budo warrior was amazing. He was capable of relating different techniques and explaining why they could work or why they couldn't. I haven't seen anyone like him, and his memory and legacy will stay with me forever.

**Q: Did he teach koBudo, too?**

A: Yes, and he was extremely knowledgeable about the history and application of each traditional weapon from Okinawa. He could relate history to technique in every weapon. He truly was an encyclopedia of knowledge.

**Q: Why did he become the leader of the itosu-kai?**

A: According to what I know, Mabuni Sensei had to leave the leadership of the style [shito-ryu] to his son. This is the Japanese tradition in Budo. Sakagami Sensei was older and senior to Mabuni's sons so Mabuni Sensei gave him the leadership of the Itosu-ha legacy that he had received from Grandmaster Itosu Anko. It was a way of allowing him to take the leadership he deserved, but Mabuni Kenwa couldn't give it to him for traditional reasons. Sakagami Sensei became the leader of the itosu-kai style of karate, but it is interesting to note that he was including the entire syllabus from naha-te and tomari-te in his teachings … not only those techniques and kata from the Itosu lineage. The teachings of Kanryo Higaonna were present in the curriculum and syllabus of Sakagami Sensei. In fact, his teachings were pretty much the same as Mabuni Kenwa's. There were no substantial differences.

# A Legacy of Excellence

And by all means, you can consider what Sakagami Ryusho Sensei was teaching as pure shito-ryu.

**Q: Do you think that it is important for a shito-ryu or itosu-kai student to know all the complete kata syllabus of the style?**

A: Not really. Each kata represents and teaches certain fighting principles. We have to look into kata using the following approach: Kata was not [originally] a set of fighting techniques. The fighting techniques were separated and they stood by themselves. Then, the old masters put them together in an organized format and created the kata. When you study the application of the movements, you must think this way and try to discover the meaning behind the technique. Sometimes you even have to reverse the kata to understand the bunkai!

Don't try to make sense of the complete kata at once because it was never meant to be that way. Pay attention to the little details in the structure of the form. There is more than meets the eye. Each kata requires time and effort to fully understand its meaning. Therefore, I think that the student in shito-ryu must learn those kata that provide him with the essence of the different flavors found in the shito-ryu style (naha, shuri and tomari) and develop an appreciation for them. Then, focus on those kata that he feels a more natural inclination to and go deep into each one of them. Study the bunkai and oyo bunkai, research the history of kata and find the true meaning behind the form. To be a master of shito-ryu doesn't necessarily mean you need to know

# SHIGERU SAWABE

60 different kata. Nobody can master this number of forms equally. Not even Mabuni Sensei had the same amount of knowledge about each single kata he knew. Instructors and professional teachers need to have an extensive knowledge of the complete kata syllabus in order to pass them onto the new generation.

**Q: Is it necessary to know different versions of the same kata to completely understand the form in all its interpretations?**

A: Let's take passai kata. According to the opinions and interpretations of the different masters, there are many different versions of this kata. We have matsumura no passai, ishimine no passai, passai dai, passai sho, et cetera. All of these are simply versions of the same. To really get the proper benefit from the form, you don't need to know all of them. Some versions are closer to others, and others are very different to the point that they can be considered a different kata all together. This doesn't really mean anything because the practitioner should take maybe two or three different versions and try to understand their origin and differences. Also, it is important to start with an easier version before learning a more complex or advanced interpretation of the same form. Teachers need to learn more to be capable of passing these different interpretations to future generations.

**Q: Are different kata used to develop specific qualities in the student's training?**

A: Definitely. That's one of the advantages of the shito-ryu style. The teacher should use specific kata to develop the student in different technical and physical areas. For instance, you don't use passai dai to develop the student's strength and body conditioning. Other forms like sanchin and tensho should be used to that effect. Each kata has its specification, and it has to be used for that specific purpose. This is one of the reasons why it seems that Mabuni Sensei used the naha-te forms in the beginning of the student's training. Maybe he used that to develop the body so he could later introduce more subtle technical actions based on speed [shuri-te]. I think that basically it all depends on the student you are teaching. The training was done in almost one-on-one situations so the teacher used to give each student specifically what he needed. This doesn't happen today, and the instruction is more mass oriented. This reduces the possibility of the instructor giving the student those things that he really needs for himself.

**Q: How does shito-ryu combine (under one format) the presentation of different styles (approaches) and fighting ideas from shuri, tomari and naha?**

A: It is a difficult question to answer because it would take hours to explain all the details, but I'll try my best to keep it short. It is clear how the format of shotokan karate works, and it is also clear how the style of goju-ryu performs the kata. Shito-ryu doesn't use any of these extremes [if we can use this term]. It makes every form more natural ... more in an Okinawan way of performing the techniques. It is not as physical and strong as shotokan, but it is neither as hard as goju. This approach is something that people understand with time. When their bodies change and they get older, the hard approach can't be used any more because it is not natural for the body. Then you have to use a more natural way of doing the kata. Let me cite an example from shotokan. In this style, the kata has been changed and designed for young and strong people. So, when they get older, they can hardly do the kata as they used to. If you look at senior instructors of hard shotokan in the past, you'll see that now they do the forms very differently. They look more natural and closer to the way shito-ryu does the forms. They even use shito-ryu kata in their curriculum now because they have realized that the approach is more natural for the body and you can use it for a long period of time. Karate was never meant to be practiced only by young people. So, in my opinion, the idea of formatting karate for strong and physically talented students was not a very good move.

# SHIGERU SAWABE

**Q: Do you separate your teaching in basic and advanced techniques in kata?**

A: Not really, because that is a mistake. I don't look at karate techniques and separate the movements into advanced and basic. There are no basic or advanced movements. Techniques are the same. Techniques are something that develop and improve with time and training. A fundamental  technique becomes "advanced," as you like to describe, when it becomes a natural movement and a reflexive reaction. An intermediate movement can counter every basic technique, and an advanced movement can easily counter every intermediate movement. What people don't understand is that any advanced movement is very easily nullified by a basic technique. Please note that when I use the terms "advanced," "intermediate" and "basic" that I'm only referring to the technical difficulty of the physical action. Simply, don't forget that the more complex the technical action is, the less likely it will be successful.

**Q: What is the difference between a sport coach and a karate teacher?**

A: Many, but unfortunately and due to the fact modern karate is moving more and more into a sportive approach, teachers are becoming like football coaches. They use the sport approach to make students better and this is wrong. On the other hand, many karate champions become instructors immediately. Dan ranks are given to competitors because they have won a tournament. Then, you have a 5th dan instructor only because he has won an international championship. How do you think this instructor will coach his students? A competitor is focused on being better and stronger himself. Usually, they don't teach the student how to be great because they still have to think about themselves. And it is actually quite normal to think about your own importance when you are young and competing. A true sensei is a differ-

# A Legacy of Excellence

ent thing all together. I have always enjoyed making my students better than me. Fortunately, young students have great teachers around the world they can go to for information, training and assistance.

**Q: In modern competition, different scores are given to different techniques. Do you agree with that idea?**

A: I like the idea of shobu-ippon because it represents what Budo is all about. One punch, and you are dead. You can't get up and keep fighting. Even if you don't put your opponent down with one single technique that is what you should strive for. Even if you don't knock him down completely, he will be in very bad shape. In this condition, there is no guarantee of victory. When you know there is only one opportunity of doing it right — because otherwise you'll be doing it wrong — you pay more attention to everything. You know that a small mistake can be fatal. You know you can score three or four more points afterward ... like in soccer. It is only one clean shot. No second chances. Like the old samurai duels. You miss, and you are killed. This is Budo, and I like this idea. Of course, it may be boring for spectators. For a Budoka who understands what is happening, however, it is very interesting. This approach influences the mental state of the fighter because of the relevance of a single action. The fighter needs to render himself empty as a mirror's polished surface reflects whatever stands before it. His mind should be empty of selfishness in an effort to react appropriately toward anything his opponent may give him. He finds himself fighting in a controlled environment, but he maintains an attitude of facing death. This is the only way we can bring true Budo spirit into modern competition without losing the traditional fighting spirit of the arts.

**Q: Is it more difficult to perform proper kicking techniques or punching techniques?**

A: Every technique has its difficulty, no matter what it may be. Personally, however, I see the necessary coordination, balance and use of all the proper lines of power in the body to be more difficult in the punching techniques. I know many people think that kicking techniques are very difficult. However, if we understand all the body mechanics involved in a simple gyaku-tsuki, we'll realize that it is extremely hard to master the correct body positioning, hip rotation, back alignment, shoulder push, torque action, et cetera. Understanding the different types of kime when punching is extremely difficult. For instance, I see many practitioners only using their arms and hips when they punch. They don't know how to use their shoulders correctly in the movement. If they did, that would fully bring the back muscles into the punch. They, because of the lack of knowledge and understanding, use too many chest muscles to compensate for the technique. They also keep the muscular tension too long after the final part of the technique. Because of this, their breath stops, which is completely incorrect.

Also, the idea of snapping your body like a whip is something that has been developed in the last decades of research. It is important to fully understand how the body works and try to get the most out of it in every physical movement.

**Q: What is the traditional model for teachers and students in Japanese karate and how do the Western students accept it?**

A: The technical model is presented to the students, and they try to copy it as accurately as possible. They have faith and confidence in the sensei, which eliminates the need for lengthy verbal discussion about the technique. The student doesn't question anything. He accepts his role and the training environment. For a Western student, all this is really strange because it is a cultural thing. They accept more personal responsibility in their own progress in the art, which compels them to continually question the structure and content of each lesson. The questions need to be answered immediately, and students are not satisfied with the Japanese answer of "because the sensei says so." Considering all these differences, it is not difficult to understand why there are sometimes misinterpretations and misunderstandings. I believe that these important cultural aspects are the key to many problems in the art of karate today. For instance, many Japanese instructors living abroad need to find a reason for every technique they teach. They also feel they have to justify everything taught in class, as this is a desperate attempt to reassure the students that they are not wasting their time. Therefore, the value of the technique is expressed in relation to the potential such techniques have for scoring points and winning tournaments.

**Q: What are the most important qualities of a good instructor?**

A: The main point is that the instructor must know himself. He must understand his strong and weak points – both physically and mentally. From there he can look to the students and try to work with the capabilities and limitations they may have. This is very basic philosophy. Only when you understand yourself can you understand other people. Without this, it is impossible to teach other people properly. Also, a good instructor keeps training himself

# A Legacy of Excellence

all the time. He doesn't stop his personal training or his learning process, and he places emphasis on the basics movements and techniques.

A good instructor should be hard and dedicated to what he does. At the same time, he has to be understanding to the student's needs and be there to help him when he needs it. This applies not only inside the dojo but outside as well. A good sensei in the traditional Budo concept is much more than a simple teacher of a fighting art.

**Q: What should an instructor be looking for in a grading session?**

A: From the technical point of view, it depends on what dan level the student is testing for. Based on this, the requirements are different. But there are basics concepts and principles the students must physically display according to the rank they are testing for; such as body control, hip action, kime, zanchin, stances and overall coordination, et cetera. These are some of the elements that every karate practitioner should have, depending, of course, on their skill level. Regardless if they pass or fail, students should present themselves with etiquette and decorum. If the attitude is wrong, I personally don't care much for the physical ability.

**Q: What is karate to you and how would you describe its benefits?**

A: Karate represents many different things. To me, it is a beautiful art that can be used as a physical activity to keep in shape and also a method of perfecting character. It is an art form, but not only because someone designed a set of

physical moves that make it look artistic. It is art because karate teaches us to use the body in a perfect way. The movements are designed to be used in the best possible way. Every single muscle and body part work together to generate the body's maximum potential in power and speed. Through the attempt to perfect these techniques, you can use your body like a tool for self-improvement. Once you have the necessary skill, that is when the true spirit of Budo must take over. Any technique, regardless of how perfect it may be from a physical point of view, is irrelevant without the correct spirit. I'm not talking about anger or rage. I am talking about good spirit, which is something creative and positive. With it, we can surpass our physical and mental limitations and improve ourselves.

**Q: Why do you think students stop training after three or four years?**

A: There is a threshold in which most of the students quit training, and this is between 1st kyu and sho-dan. After this period of time [three or four years], the student is not motivated any more because the initial illusion has gone away. Now the students realize that to progress there is only one way to go ... constant repetition of what they have learned and this becomes a boring chore. Another reason is that their technical foundation hasn't been set properly, and they start to see their own limitations and get disappointed. If they don't have a precise understanding of the art and basics from the very beginning, it is impossible for them to keep motivated to progress. They simply have no desire to stick to it. In the Japanese culture, the student is not supposed to enjoy the training. Training is a challenge and something difficult the student has to face every day. It is not a hobby or a pleasure as it is in the Western world.

# A Legacy of Excellence

**Q: For decades you kept an excellent relationship with Fumio Demura Sensei and eventually served as an advisor to him. What can you tell us about your relationship with him?**

A: I know Demura Sensei since he was a young man and started training at Sakagami Sensei's dojo. He was a very dedicated student and always had the correct attitude of a budoka. I remember him training hard and never quit regardless of how tired he was or how hard the training session was. It seemed to me that he had – even at theearly days – a "mission" to accomplish. The offer from Dan Ivan Sensei was not presented yet at that time but the young Fumio was determined to make something big with his life.

**Q: Did you keep in touch with mih when he moved to the U.S.?**

A: Yes, I did. I remember that it was hard for him in the beginning but his determination made him to overcome all the obstacles and show the world that there were other ways to promote and expand the art of karate and maintain the tradition and the Budo values at the same time.

**Q: Did you advise him when he was in the U.S.?**

A: Yes. We talked often and I always advised him. He knew I understodd his position and how things were developing in the U.S. and in Japan. He left Japan at a young age, made a name for himself and developed a reputation around the world. Sometimes these things are not well accepted by the older generation but I always encouraged him to pursue his own path and to do what was best for him.

**Q: Finally, what advice would you give to all karate-do practitioners, regardless of style?**

A: My advice is to keep practicing all the time. Even if you feel tired, bored and with no motivation whatsoever … keep doing it. You'll understand one day. Because the more you practice, the more you understand when the right time comes. Never neglect the basics and take the kata training seriously. Never forsake one kata for another and treat them all the same because they bring different benefits to you. Dedicate yourself to your instructor. When you become a teacher, teach anyone who is willing to learn. Karate teaches you how to gain and keep control of any situation in life. When you face a difficult task, push yourself into it until you can do it. Don't give up under pressure. Keep a good attitude and strong discipline.

# MASTERSCLASS KOBUDO

### By Fumio Demura

**NUNCHAKU** - The nunchaku consists of two pieces of wood of various lengths that are joined together by rope (originally horse hair) or a chain (originally the "bit" from a horse's bridle) to create a formidable weapon of self-defense. Audiences are consistently impressed with martial artists' dazzling and innovative routines using the nunchaku. In this video, Fumio Demura sensei teaches proper grips, stances, swings, strikes, blocks and a basic beginner's kata. (Approx. 52 min.) **US$24.95 - ISBN: 978-1-933901-94-7**

**KAMA** - The kama is a sickle that Okinawan farmers used to harvest their rice crops. Unlike other tools such as the bo and sai—which are normally made of wood or bamboo—the kama has a sharp cutting edge. In this video, Fumio Demura sensei teaches the fundamentals of proper kama use, including proper grips, strikes, stances, counters and defenses. (Approx. 58 min.) **US$24.95 - ISBN: 978-1-933901-95-4**

**TONFA** - Originally adapted from an Okinawan farm implement, martial artists today use the tonfa to perform kata (techniques) and as a weapon. Former national free-fighting champion from Japan, a member of the Black Belt Hall of Fame and tonfa authority, Fumio Demura teaches proper grips, strikes, stances, defense moves, attacks and other techniques that will improve your overall skill and coordination. (Approx. 46 min.)
**US$24.95 - ISBN: 978-1-933901-96-1**

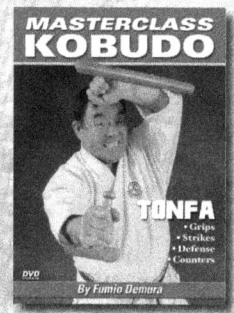

**BO** - Fumio Demura studied under Japanese master Ryusho Sakagami and Okinawan master Kenshin Taira. Demura has won the All-Japan Karate Freefighting Championships (1961), twice been voted into the Black Belt Hall of Fame and is recognized the world over as one of the premier martial artists of all time. Bo features grasping, striking, blocking, kata, maneuvering and application. (Approx. 60 min.) **US$24.95 - ISBN: 978-1-933901-97-8**

**SAI** - Fumio Demura studied under Japanese master Ryusho Sakagami and Okinawan master Kenshin Taira. Demura has won the All-Japan Karate Freefighting Championships (1961), twice been voted into the Black Belt Hall of Fame and is recognized the world over as one of the premier martial artists of all time. Sai features proper grips, attacks, defense, kata, maneuvering and application. (Approx. 60 min.) **US$24.95 - ISBN: 978-1-933901-98-5**

**EKU** - The eku bo—also known as the kai—is an oar used by Okinawan fishermen. Most of the techniques for using the eku bo are much like those of the bo, another Okinawan weapon. In this video, Fumio Demura sensei covers basic stances, proper grips, defense movements, blocks and counters. A basic "beginner's" kata is also covered in this volume. (Approx. 54 min.)
**US$24.95 - ISBN: 978-1-933901-99-2**

## ORDER NOW
### www.martialartsdigital.com

# MASTERSCLASS SHITO RYU KARATE

**By Fumio Demura**

**Volume 1** includes striking points, target areas, standing positions and hand, elbow, kicking and blocking techniques; basic sparring and self-defense. (Approx. 90 min.) **US$24.95 - ISBN: 978-1-933901-89-3**

**Volume 2** includes body dynamics, flexibility training, self-defense training, blocks, stances, striking, leg techniques, sparring and five kata. (Approx. 60 min.) **US$24.95 - ISBN: 978-1-933901-90-9**

**Volume 3** includes senior and black-belt-level kata and self-defense techniques; judo throws; punches, elbows, chops, kicks and other techniques; and kata (naifanchin shodan, matsumura rohai, sanchin, jitte, bassai dai and jiin). (Approx. 60 min.)
**US$24.95 - ISBN: 978-1-933901-91-6**

**Volume 4** includes special breathing exercises; sparring drills; unsoku, bunkai and oyo; and black-belt-level kata (naifanchin nidan, jion, niseishi [nijushi ho], wanshu [empi], kusankui dai [kosukun dai] and wankan). (Approx. 60 min.) **US$24.95 - ISBN: 978-1-933901-92-3**

**Volume 5** includes how to develop bigger, better and more powerful kicking techniques; black-belt-level drills; self-defense techniques; and kata (naifanchin san dan, seienshin, aoyagi [men's version], aoyagi [women's version], seipai and juroku). (Approx. 60 min.)
**US$24.95 - ISBN: 978-1-933901-93-0**

# ORDER NOW
www.martialartsdigital.com

*NOTES*

www.ingramcontent.com/pod-product-compliance
Lightning Source LLC
Chambersburg PA
CBHW061801070526
44586CB00023B/2658